ALSO BY DR. BOB ROTELLA

BOOKS:

Golf Is Not a Game of Perfect
Parenting Your Superstar
Scientific Foundations of Coaching
Psychological Foundations of Sport
Mind Mastery for Winning Golf
Mind, Set and Match

AUDIO TAPES:

Golfing Out of Your Mind
Putting Out of Your Mind

CD-ROM PROGRAMS:

Lower Your Score (with Tom Kite)

GOLF IS
A GAME OF
CONFIDENCE

DR. BOB ROTELLA

with Bob Cullen

SIMON & SCHUSTER

SIMON & SCHUSTER

ROCKEFELLER CENTER

1230 AVENUE OF THE AMERICAS

NEW YORK, NY 10020

DESIGNED BY BARBARA M. BACHMAN

MANUFACTURED IN THE UNITED STATES OF AMERICA

7 9 10 8

LIBRARY OF CONGRESS CATALOGING-IN-PUBLICATION DATA

ROTELLA, ROBERT J.

GOLF IS A GAME OF CONFIDENCE / BOB ROTELLA WITH BOB CULLEN.

P.   CM.

1. GOLF—PSYCHOLOGICAL ASPECTS.   I. CULLEN, BOB.   II. TITLE.

GV979.P75R65   1996

796.352′01′9—dc20   96-16783

CIP

ISBN 0-684-83040-X

To my brother, Guy. Thanks for letting me play with

the big kids. Thanks for showing me the importance

of education. And thanks for being a great editor.

Contents

Introduction

GOLFERS SOMETIMES ASK ME FOR MY DEFINITION OF CONFIDENCE. I've been fortunate enough to spend more than twenty years working with athletes as a head coach, a trainer of the mind. For about a dozen of those years, I've been teaching and coaching professional golfers. Here is one of the best definitions I've come up with:

Confidence is playing with your eyes.

I hear this from athletes in all sports with targets. Think of the shooter on a roll in basketball. She just looks at the basket and lets it go. Think of a great pitcher when he's sharp. He looks at the catcher's mitt and throws it in there. Think of the trap shooter. He squints at the clay disc and squeezes the trigger.

The eye of the confident athlete zeroes in on the objective. The brain and the rest of the body simply react. The basketball shooter doesn't give herself a lecture on the mechanics of pushing a ball through the air. The pitcher doesn't mentally rehearse the motions of shoulder, arm, elbow, wrist, and finger that produce a slider. The trap shooter needn't ponder how to coordinate the movements of his torso and his trigger finger.

Confident athletes let their brains and nervous systems perform the skills they have rehearsed and mastered—without interference from the conscious mind.

So it should be with the golfer. The confident golfer sees where he wants the ball to go. Sometimes, even after he turns his eyes back to the ball, he continues to see the target with his "mind's eye." He lets his body swing the club. The more confident he is, the better the chance the ball will go there.

I don't know why this is so. I know only that this is the way the human organism was created to function and the way it functions best.

Of course, if everyone were endowed with an abundant, constant supply of confidence, my profession would not exist. But not everyone is.

Most golfers experience confidence only occasionally and only haphazardly. They normally play in a state of barely repressed tension. Their swings and scores reflect it. But now and again, for reasons they do not understand, things fall into place. They hit a couple of good shots, sink a putt or two, and suddenly they feel confident. They begin playing with their eyes, hitting the ball to the target, and they experience golf on an entirely different level. They string pars and birdies together. They glimpse their potential as golfers.

Inevitably, though, the swing falls out of the slot, or a couple of putts slide by the hole, and the spell of confidence ends. These golfers do not control its departure, any more than they control the passing of a thunderstorm over the course. They finish their rounds with their old golf games, warm but wistful memories of their hot streaks, and a gnawing sense of frustration.

The golfers I work with refuse to wait until confidence descends upon them. Most of them are professionals whose dreams and livelihoods depend on finding a way to play confidently. Some are amateurs, from scratch players to high handicappers, who simply want to play golf as well as they can. They understand that this requires confidence.

In all sports, confidence separates winners from also-rans. The best athletes combine confidence with physical competence. But every smart coach I've ever known, if he has to choose between a competent athlete who lacks confidence and an athlete of lesser physical gifts whose mind is ready to maximize his potential, who is confident, will pick the confident player.

I teach all golfers that they are endowed with free will. They can control their thoughts. In fact, they are responsible for their thoughts. They can choose to think confidently. They can take this confidence with them every time they go to the golf course, and they can have it from their first swing to their last.

But it takes an honest commitment to develop confidence.

I have found that simply stating this premise does not persuade a lot of people. They are not accustomed to thinking the way great golfers think. They can't believe confidence is something they can learn and control.

Some of them, in truth, see confidence as a form of self-deception. I frequently meet people who tell me that dwelling on thoughts of what they want to happen—another good definition of confidence—is unrealistic. To me, they've just found a rationalization for the thoughts that defeat them.

I believe that confident thinking, about golf or anything else, is just being honest about where you're capable of going. It at least gives you a chance to find out what you can attain.

Some golfers tell me it's too hard to stay positive and confident. They may try it for a while, but they give it up when they run into adversity.

I reply that it may seem easier to be negative in the short run. But in the long run you're going to waste a lot more energy being negative. You'll flail away at the game, but you'll never find out how good you could have been. So the truth of the matter is, if you intend to invest time and energy in golf, it's a lot easier to be positive.

I've found that stories teach more effectively than do lectures on theory. So I've assembled eighteen stories about players I have known and worked with: eighteen holes, if you will, of a golf course. Some of these players have recorded extraordinary achievements in major championships, like the 8 and 7 thrashing Paul Runyan administered to the great Sam Snead in the 1938 PGA or the 66 Davis Love shot in the final round of the 1995 Masters. Some have just broken 90 or 80 for the first time. These accomplishments, to them, were just as sweet as Davis's 66.

These eighteen golfers have two things in common. They love the game. And they all have something to teach you about confidence, about playing with your eyes.

No. 1

How Brad Faxon

Stayed in the Present

THE FIRST HOLE AT THE RIVIERA COUNTRY CLUB IN LOS ANGELES presents a lot of choices. It's a great starting hole, a 501-yard par five. The tee sits eighty feet above the fairway, giving the player a panoramic view of the verdant canyon where the course is situated. For the members, this elevation provides the comforting assurance that the first shot will at least get up in the air. And it means that even if their first couple of strokes are hit with irons or fairway woods, are the product of stiff muscles, and don't go particularly far, they still have a chance to reach the green in regulation and get started with a par.

But to Brad Faxon, standing on that elevated tee at the beginning of the last round of the 1995 PGA Championship, No. 1 looked much more challenging. Brad had played well the first three days of the tournament, getting to five strokes under par. But some twenty golfers had played better; the leader, Ernie Els, was eleven strokes ahead. Brad wants to play well in all the tournaments he enters, particularly majors, but the 1995 PGA was especially important. It was the last opportunity to earn points for the Ryder Cup team, and Brad had been dreaming of playing in the Ryder Cup for a long time. As the tournament began, he was fourteenth in the standings, a few hundred points away from the top ten and a spot on the team. The math was complicated, and nothing would be settled until the last strokes had been played Sunday. But in essence, the situation was simple. To earn enough points to make the team, Brad had to play not just an excellent round but a superb one, a round that would vault him past at least a dozen players and into the top five.

He faced, in short, one of the great challenges of the game. Could he produce his best golf when he most wanted to produce it?

Brad and the thousands of spectators in the canyon below knew that if he were to make the Ryder Cup team, he could hardly afford to start with a comfortable par on No. 1. He wanted to birdie the hole, to eagle it if possible. Doing that would require a long, accurate drive off the tee. But using the driver would bring into play the out-of-bounds stakes that line the left side of the hole and the trees that line the right. He would have to hit the fairway, because trying to reach the green in two from the thick kikuyu grass rough was foolhardy. Without backspin, the ball would never hold the green. So his driver would have to be hit nearly perfectly. It would have to be hit with confidence.

FORTUNATELY, BRAD HAD been preparing to hit that driver for a long time. When I first started working with him, in the late 1980s, he was a young player with a deft short game and an extraordinary mind. Brad is one of the most enthusiastic, optimistic, and playful human beings I have ever encountered. He loves playing games of all kinds, and he is very creative. But he lacked confidence in his driver. When he mishit a wedge or a putt, as even the best players do, he had no trouble forgetting it and believing that the next shot would go in. But when he sprayed a drive off the tee, he felt as if all the energy had been sucked out of his body. Thereafter, the club felt suspect in his hands.

We worked for several years on this problem. To begin with, Brad hit a lot of 3-woods off tees where his fellow competitors hit drivers, sacrificing distance for the sake of confidence. He worked with a swing instructor to fix some minor flaws in his mechanics. He worked at developing the discipline to savor and remember his good drives and the patience to wait as his driving improved. Gradually, he became more confident, and in 1992, he broke through to win twice and finish eighth on the money list. He still was, and probably always will be, most confident with a wedge or putter in his hands. Even the best players find that certain facets of the game come easily to them; they must work at trusting others. But Brad had begun to relish hitting his driver again.

And Brad had done some intelligent things to prepare himself during the week of the PGA. Several times, after leaving the course, he met some friends and went Rollerblading alongside the beaches from Santa Monica to Muscle Beach and Venice— as much as twenty miles round trip. It's probably safe to assume that Bobby Jones, Ben Hogan, and Jack Nicklaus never went Rollerblading during the week of a major championship. It's not a traditional form of golf preparation. But Brad likes the exercise, he likes the fresh air, and he likes the company of the friends he makes in abundance as he travels the circuit. And he's good enough to be confident that he won't fall and hurt himself. Most important, Rollerblading is fun; it relaxes him.

In my experience, a player who spends every minute at a tournament site, beating balls and worrying, trying to grind his way to a peak performance, is likely to do worse than the player who looks at preparation as a long-term process, who gets in a reasonable amount of practice at the tournament site, and then finds a way to relax and forget about golf.

Brad also chose to dwell on thoughts that would help him. He had not played particularly well in the weeks preceding the tournament. He started well in the British Open, but finished fifteenth. Then he went home to New England to play in the New England Classic. By chance, he was paired the first two days with Lanny Wadkins, the Ryder Cup captain. He wanted very much to impress Wadkins, and he put a lot of extra pressure on himself. He missed the cut. He made the cut the next week, at the Buick Open, but he finished back in the pack. Nevertheless, as he headed to California, Brad thought he was playing well. He simply wasn't pulling his game together and scoring.

Fortunately, he's always liked Riviera. It's a course whose holes are visible; there are no blind shots. The architect, George Thomas, believed in confronting a player with challenges rather than surprising him. Brad feels most comfortable on a tee that helps him visualize the shape of the shot he wants to hit, and at Riviera, the design clearly suggests fades on some holes and draws on others. He reminded himself that he likes the course.

The Riviera greens were still soft from a partly successful reconstruction job during the previous year. Brad knew that they were bound to spike up, and that lots of players would gripe about it. He decided to think of that as an advantage. If he could will himself to take the greens as he found them, without complaint, he would have a huge advantage over all the players who would whine, moan, and convince themselves that the condition of the greens meant they weren't going to make any putts.

As we often do, Brad and I took a walk together on the eve of the tournament's final round. This time, it was a short walk, up a staircase at the home of a friend, Peter Lomenzo, to a little deck with a bench and a view of the Pacific. We sat and talked. He knows by now that there are no magic words, no parlor tricks that a sports psychologist can perform to put a player into the right frame of mind before a crucial round. He knows that there are no startling new breakthroughs in behavioral science that I can reveal to help him to play better. He knows, and even enjoys, the fact that our conversation will revolve around two basic and interrelated ideas that we have discussed many times before. One is staying in the present. The second is committing to the process. A large part of this book will be devoted to elaborating on those two ideas.

Staying in the present sounds simple, so simple that even some teaching professionals can't understand how it can be difficult. I did a clinic recently for PGA members in the Boston area. One of them raised his hand and asked a question.

"What's the big deal about staying in the present?" he wanted to know. "How can it be hard for tour players to keep their minds in the present on Sunday?"

I asked him whether he played many tournaments himself. He said no. I asked what his name was. Let's say that he said "Joe."

"Okay, Joe," I continued. "Who do you think is the sexiest woman in America?"

Without hesitating much, he named Cindy Crawford.

"Wow, Joe," I said. "What an incredible coincidence! As I was leaving my hotel this morning, the phone rang and it was Cindy. She told me you'd be at my workshop today. She wanted me to tell you that she wants very much to meet you afterwards. She's in room 201, and she said that precisely at seven o'clock, she'll be slipping out of her bath and into something more comfortable. That's when she wants you to be there. She wants to take maybe half an hour for a little conversation, and then from seven-thirty till ten, she wants to make mad, passionate love to you."

Joe was blushing.

"But there's one catch, Joe," I went on. "If at anytime between now and seven-thirty you think about her, the deal's off."

"That's impossible," Joe managed to say.

"And you've only been thinking about Cindy for five minutes," I replied. "These guys have been dreaming about winning golf tournaments for most of their lives."

Then they began to understand the mental discipline a successful tour golfer needs to stay in the present.

To play golf as well as he can, a player has to focus his mind tightly on the shot he is playing now, in the present.

If the golfer thinks about anything else, that pure reaction between the eye and the brain and the nervous system is polluted. Performance usually suffers. This is just the way human beings are constructed.

A player can't think about what happened to the last shot he hit, or the shot he played with the tournament on the line a week ago. That's thinking about the past. He can't think about how great it would be to win the tournament, or how terrible it would feel to blow it. That's thinking about the future.

In Brad's case, I told him on that Saturday night, it meant that it would do him no good to think about how badly he had played with Lanny Wadkins in New England two weeks previously, or how very few putts had fallen for him during the first three rounds at Riviera. That was the past.

Most especially, it would do him no good to think about making the Ryder Cup team, or the fact that he'd probably need to shoot in the low 60s to do it. That would be thinking about results, the future.

He already knew that there was no way he could decide simply to ignore the Ryder Cup. All summer, interest in the team had been building. The point standings were posted in every locker room; at every tour stop, reporters asked the players in contention how they felt about it. The Ryder Cup was an unavoidable distraction of the type that tour players have to learn to cope with.

Brad and I had already agreed that there was no way he could avoid thinking about the Ryder Cup from time to time. But he couldn't afford to think about it on the golf course. If Ryder Cup thoughts occurred to him while he was competing, he had to catch himself, stop, and return his mind to the present, to the shot at hand.

Brad had resolved to turn the Ryder Cup hubbub into an asset instead of a distraction. Every time someone asked him about it, he would answer that, yes, he wanted to make the team; as he did so, he would remind himself that his best chance of doing that lay in keeping his mind in the present, focused on the shot ahead, every time he competed.

Throughout the week of the PGA, he made certain to avoid falling into the trap of trying to calculate where he stood in relation to the other players with a chance to make the team and what he would have to shoot to beat them. Trying to sort that out would have taken his mind so far afield that he might never have found his way back. When he teed off on Sunday morning, he was deliberately unaware of what place he was in.

I told Brad on that Saturday evening that he was doing everything right with his mind. He just had to be patient and trust that the results would come. I told him that his goal ought to be simple: to be able to stand in front of the mirror on Sunday night with a big grin on his face, able to tell himself that he had trusted his swing all day, that he had had fun playing a meaning-ful round of golf.

And then I said good-bye and got ready to catch an early flight from Los Angeles on Sunday morning. One of the great things about golf is that once a player steps onto the first tee, no coach, no swing doctor, and no sports psychologist can help him. He is alone with his mind and his caddie. He has to do it himself. I watched on television what Brad did in the last round of the PGA.

STANDING ON THE first tee, Brad told me later, he immersed his mind in the process of hitting good shots. The process varies from player to player. Some players visualize the shots they want to hit and see everything about them—the flight, the trajec-tory, the bounce, and the roll—in their mind's eye. Some play-ers don't visualize. They simply identify a target, then think about the ball going there. Others just look at the target and react.

But a player who is committed to the process of hitting good shots will never draw a club back until he knows where he wants the ball to go and believes that the club in his hands will send it there.

Good players typically have a physical routine wrapped around this mental process to make sure their alignment and posture are consistently correct. Physical routines can vary. Brad, for example, sometimes takes a practice swing and some-times doesn't. But the mental routine at the heart of the process cannot vary.

Brad had, in fact, been thinking about the first drive since going to bed Saturday night. He had seen the shot he wanted over and over again. He stepped up, addressed the ball, and replicated the shot he had seen in his mind. The ball flew straight and far, hung up against the sky, and then dropped into the middle of the fairway, three hundred yards out. He felt a surge of excitement as he walked down the hill to the fairway below.

Brad's caddie, Cubby Burke, set the bag on the fairway and gave him the yardage. He had 195 yards to carry the big sand bunker that guarded the front right portion of the green, where the hole was cut. He had 201 yards to the hole. The wind, as it generally does at Riviera, was coming off the nearby Pacific, blowing softly from right to left.

It would, Brad knew, be a 4-iron shot under normal conditions. But these were not normal conditions. He could feel the adrenaline pumping. His first instinct was to hit a hard 5-iron, with a draw, right over the trap.

Just to see what Cubby thought, Brad asked him.

"Solid four," Cubby suggested.

Brad knew Cubby couldn't tell how excited he felt, how strong.

"Cub, I'm going to hit a hard draw, with a five," he said.

"Well," said Cubby, pulling out the 5-iron. "See your shot. You know what you want to do with it."

This is one reason why Cubby is a good caddie. Some caddies take great pride in their job of measuring yardage and recommending clubs, so much so that when the golfer wants to go against their recommendations, they argue. Cubby knows that the best thing he can do for Brad is to help him feel decisive before every shot. He said the right thing.

Brad went through his process again and swung. The shot was flawless, exactly as Brad had envisioned it, a shot that started high, drew into the pin, and cleared the bunker with a few yards to spare. It rolled to a stop about fifteen feet past the hole.

Walking onto the green, Brad was pleased. The putting surface had dried out and firmed up somewhat since Saturday. A mid-iron that carried the bunker and reached the green was bound to roll some. He had put it about as close to the pin as he possibly could.

Now he faced an eagle putt. If there was one thing Brad had found fault with in his play for the first few days, it was his putting. He had not, he felt, been free enough.

When I speak of a player being loose and free on the putting green, I don't mean careless. But most players err in the other direction. They don't trust their instincts and abilities. They doubt whether they've read the green correctly. They try to force the clubhead to stay on line. They try to steer the ball into the hole. They putt worse by being too careful than they would if they were careless.

When Brad is putting well, he comes close to having the ideal mind. He never thinks about speed. He feels that thinking about speed is like thinking about how far to throw a ball when you're playing catch. The outcome is likely to be an awkward toss. In the same way, thoughts like "Don't run it too far past" or "Get it there" lead to lots of three-putts.

Brad's putting process starts with a thorough examination of the green. On a day when he is particularly sharp, he can see at a glance things that most golfers would never notice—the grain, how closely the grass has been cut, patches where the grass is a few millimeters longer than others. He gauges the slope. Sometimes he gets Cubby's input. He is looking for the line on which the ball will roll into the hole. As soon as he thinks he has that line, he steps over the ball, makes a practice swing or two if he feels the need for it, and then lets the putt go, trusting his first instincts.

Once he's over a putt, Brad doesn't think specifically about getting the ball into the hole. He's already picked out a line that he's convinced will do that. He concentrates narrowly on the task at hand—getting the ball rolling well on the line he has selected. Then he waits to see what happens, letting the green take care of everything else. He knows that when his mind is right, his system and his senses will take care of touch and direction much better than he would if he tried consciously to control those variables.

Conversely, when a golfer thinks about results instead of process, the mind doesn't know where the hole is.

On the first hole at Riviera, Brad's eagle putt went right into the hole.

He was on his way. And he was brimming with confidence.

Some people might say that it's easy to be confident when you've just holed an eagle putt. But what if the putt had missed?

To be sure, success breeds confidence. But great players don't depend on success at the first green for their confidence. They strive to maintain the same attitude whether or not the first putt falls. Brad, for instance, deliberately avoids measuring how well he is putting by how many putts fall. He knows that too many variables, some of them beyond his control, can influence that. He tries to monitor whether he is putting confidently and getting the ball rolling well on his intended line. If he does that, and the ball comes close to the hole, he feels that he is putting well. If the first one or two don't fall, he believes that only increases the chances that the third or fourth ones will.

Still, it was great to nail that first putt.

No. 2 at Riviera is the toughest hole on the course, a 460-yard par four that calls for a long fade off the tee and a long iron second shot to a narrow green. Again, Brad shaped his shots just as he envisioned them. But this time his 22-foot birdie putt ran just past the edge.

At the third, Brad again drove into the fairway. This time, he found himself somewhere between a 7-iron and a 6-iron. Without much thought, he asked for the six. Brad was playing by feel, trusting his instincts. His instincts at No. 1 had told him to take less club, to hit the hard 5-iron. At No. 3, they told him to hit a little six and not to work the ball, to go straight for the pin over a bunker.

Brad was smart enough to trust himself and go with his instincts. He knows that being trusting and decisive have more to do with the success of a shot than calibrating the distance. Almost invariably, a player's second thought about club selection is based on doubt. Predictably enough, it rarely works as well as the first idea.

Brad's 6-iron went dead straight and stopped five feet from the hole. His playing partner, Jose Maria Olazabal, was a foot outside him, and Brad got a good read from watching Olazabal's putt.

Lining up that putt, for the first time that day he let his mind wander from the present. He thought, for a moment, that if he made the putt he would be three under after just three holes, off to a brilliant start.

Some people have the impression that players with great minds never experience distracting thoughts, doubts, or fears. As a matter of fact, they do. Brad is no exception. Players with great minds don't stay in the present on every shot; they only strive to. The good ones constantly monitor themselves and catch themselves when their minds start to wander. This is what Brad did. He reminded himself to get back into his putting process. He used a physical cue—lining up the "Tour Balata" line on his Titleist with the line on which he intended to roll the putt. And he knocked it in.

He parred the fourth, a 230-yard par three. At the fifth tee, he pulled out his 3-wood to play a 419-yard par four.

This choice suggests the difference between a confident player and a reckless player. Brad was hitting his driver beautifully; there was no question about his confidence. But No. 5 is a tight hole, with out-of-bounds right and trees left. Brad was playing with a game plan, and the plan called for a 3-wood. He had the discipline to stick with his plan.

We'll consider game plans in more detail later on. Suffice it to say now that a good game plan helps a player to swing confidently and decisively, because he knows he's already made the most rational, intelligent strategy choices.

He hooked his tee shot at No. 5, into the first cut of rough. But the 3-wood did its job, leaving him short of more serious trouble and able to play a 7-iron into the green, which he did, leaving himself a 30-foot putt. Brad had not been making many 30-footers during the tournament, but as he lined this one up, he was thinking he was due to make one. He got the ball rolling on his intended line and at the last moment, it dove left, into the hole. He was four under for the day.

No. 6 is Riviera's signature hole, a 175-yard par three with a little pot bunker in the middle of the green. In practice, this means that the hole has alternate greens, one to the left of the bunker and one to the right. The pin on this day was back left. Brad could immediately see the perfect shot—a 6-iron, starting at the left edge of the pot bunker and drawing in toward the flag. He hit it and left himself a 15-foot putt with a right-to-left break.

The cup, he could see, was cut into a slope. And the green looked shaggier to him. He sensed that this putt would be a little slower than the previous ones. Again, he hit it perfectly. Again, it went in.

That birdie brought some new potential distractions. The crowd roared, and he could see that his gallery was beginning to swell. He glanced at a leader board and saw that his name was on it. He had jumped from five under to ten under, and he had moved up into the middle of the top ten.

I don't generally recommend that players look at leader boards during a round. I think it takes them out of the present and diverts their minds into thoughts about results, outcomes, and other things that can do them no good. But some players look at them anyway; sometimes they're unavoidable. I tell them that if they're going to do it, they had better be prepared to ward off any distraction and return to the kind of thinking that got their names up there to begin with.

I'm not the only one who recomends this, and golf is not the only sport where it's a good idea. A couple of years ago, I was in Phoenix with Billy Mayfair, and we had sideline passes to the Fiesta Bowl. Notre Dame fell behind in the first half. We listened to what Lou Holtz told the team at halftime.

"Okay, guys, I don't want anyone looking at the scoreboard," Holtz said.

The principle is the same.

As THE RIVIERA crowd roared, Brad could feel his body responding, starting to feel more nervous and excited. At the same time, he felt acutely sensitive to everything around him. He hit a 3-wood off the tee at No. 7, a 408-yard par four, and left himself 151 yards to the pin. The wind was at his back and he felt strong. He hit a 9-iron. So sharp was his feel for the ball that while it was in the air, he thought it might be a bit short, and he said "go" to it. It landed three feet short of the hole. The putt had a six-inch break. Brad knew better than to linger over it, to think too much, and to get careful. He stroked it in.

Now the crowd was big and loud, and his friends in the gallery were screaming. He could see people who had been watching other pairings streaming toward the eighth tee. He felt buoyed by the noise and excitement.

Brad, again following his game plan, pulled out a 3-wood. No. 8 is a tight 370-yard par 4 with overhanging trees blocking approaches from the right edge of the fairway. Brad played down the left side, but he hit the ball a little too hard. He was in the rough with a decent lie, but without much chance to spin his approach.

His wedge flew up from the rough, wobbled a little in the air, and bounced once in the kikuyu rough before rolling onto the green and stopping eight feet from the hole. The crowd roared, thinking that Brad had planned it that way.

Now distractions were assaulting Brad's mind. He thought that making the putt would move him to seven under for the day, and perhaps into the tournament's top five. Not coincidentally, for the first time that day, he overread a putt. He played a break that wasn't there, and the ball slid by the hole.

He walked to the ninth tee. Spectators clapped him on the back, told him how well he was doing. The breeze was again at his back and he aimed his drive at the pair of bunkers that guard the fairway. Someone in the crowd told the ball to hurry, but Brad knew there was no need. His ball carried about 280 yards, well over both bunkers, and left him between a 9-iron and a wedge to the green. He hit the 9-iron about twenty-five feet past the hole.

He had another birdie putt, and now he could not ignore the physical symptoms of nerves. His fingers and hands were tingling. The yelling of the crowd rang in his ears.

I teach players to welcome these nervous symptoms rather than fear them. They work and practice all their lives to make it to a situation like the one Brad was in, a situation that gets the adrenaline flowing. Nerves will only make them choke if they fear the symptoms and start to focus their attention on their hands rather than on their targets, if they start to worry and wonder why their hands are shaking. Once they do that, players tend to tell themselves that they can't putt with shaking hands. They have to remember that lots of tournaments have been won by players in that condition.

Brad welcomed his symptoms, and rolled the birdie putt. It seemed to have missed, but it was breaking so sharply at the end that it half turned around and fell in at the top of the hole.

The crowd, in this situation at a major championship, becomes part of the action. It emitted a roar unlike any Brad had ever heard for himself. He jabbed at the sky with his fist. He got goose bumps. His heart started to pound. He had gone out in 28 strokes. It was the lowest nine-hole total ever in a major championship.

As Brad walked off the green, spectators yelled things like "Ryder Cup!" and "59!" Someone close to the path where the players walk got in his face and said, "You could win this thing."

Fortunately, Brad has always liked playing for a gallery. He has spent his entire career making friends with the people who watch him play; as a consequence, the fans almost always are pulling for him. Some players find that a big crowd makes them want to avoid mistakes, avoid being ridiculed. A big crowd turns Brad into an entertainer. He feeds off its energy.

But he had to be careful not to let the gallery's support turn his mind away from the present. There was more than enough temptation to do that in any case. As Brad made the turn, the leaders were just starting their round, passing by him on adjoining fairways. As he glanced at them, the notion that he could win the tournament flashed through his mind.

Brad worked hard not to get carried away by the excitement. At No. 10, a 315-yard par four, he opted for a 3-iron off the tee, because the wind was not helping him, although he knew that some of the big hitters would try to drive the green. His sand wedge second from 80 yards out in the fairway was 10 feet short of the hole, and he missed his birdie putt.

At No. 11, the wind was behind him and he decided to try to reach the green, 564 yards away, in two shots. His drive was perfect, finding the narrow landing area about 285 yards out. He crushed a 3-wood that carried 245 yards and bounced up to the green. The eagle putt stayed out this time, but the birdie pulled him to eight under for the day and 13 under for the tournament.

Now he let his thoughts edge ahead of himself. After two strong shots at No. 12, he had an eight-foot birdie putt. But as he told me later, with his characteristic humor, "I thought about a bunch of other things—going to nine under, winning the tournament, my acceptance speech."

The hard fact is, any player on the back nine who's thinking about his acceptance speech is not likely to have a chance to deliver it. He pulled the birdie putt, missing by four inches. The crowd gasped as if the putt had just missed, but Brad knew he had hit it badly. Four inches on an eight-foot putt is a canyon-sized miss for a player of his caliber.

Then he did the only thing he could do in the circumstances. He quietly laughed at himself for allowing all the extraneous influences to affect him. And he began working to draw his attention back to where it had to be.

He did a good job parring Nos. 13 and 14, and now there were two conflicting thoughts running through his mind. *Don't,* he told himself, *let a couple of missed birdie putts discourage you. Stay with the process. Stay in the present.* But at the same time, he was thinking that he had only four holes left. He needed some birdies to make a run at the championship.

No. 15 is one of the toughest holes on the back side, a 447-yard dogleg right. Still feeling powerful, Brad blew his drive right over the fairway bunker that marks the dogleg's turn. Though in previous rounds he had been hitting 3-irons and 4-irons into the green, he had only a 6-iron left. But he had the wind in his face and a hanging lie, with the ball above his feet, the kind of situation that promotes a hook. He pushed any thought of a hook out of his mind and decided instead to hit what he calls a "punch-and-hold fade" into the breeze. It went where his mind had envisioned it, leaving him a 15-foot birdie putt.

His putting stroke faltered here, and he hit the putt too hard. It was the first putt of the day, he would recall, that felt wrong leaving the putter. But his mental mistake came on the second putt, a three-footer, downhill, with a small break to the right. He had a clump of spike marks between his ball and the hole, and he thought about the spike marks instead of trusting his stroke. He missed, and made bogey.

Players sometimes tell me that they can't trust their putting stroke if they see spike marks on their line. When they do, I put a putter shaft down on the green, across their line, and ask them to putt over it. If they hit the ball just a little harder than normal, it jumps over the shaft and goes in the hole. Even then, some will say the putter shaft is round and a spike mark isn't. So I'll take a nickel and stand it in the turf and make them putt through that. They generally can. Spike marks don't deflect putts off line nearly as often as they deflect players' minds from the trusting state they ought to be in.

Now Brad faced yet another challenge to his mental discipline. When a player in the midst of a hot round hits a bad shot or two and makes a bogey or worse, all sorts of useless thoughts are liable to flit through his mind: *There goes 59.* Or *There goes the Ryder Cup.* Or *How could I have missed that putt?* All of those are thoughts focused on the past. The only useful thought for Brad to entertain at that moment was about where he wanted to hit his tee shot on No. 16.

As he walked to the tee, buoyed by the continuing applause and encouragement from the gallery, Brad tried to do that. *Don't let the bogey distract you from what you're supposed to do,* he told himself. *You can still hit a good shot here.*

Which is what Brad did. No. 16 is an old-fashioned kind of island green par three, the kind virtually surrounded by sand. Brad hit a 7-iron with a draw that checked up about twenty-five feet short of the hole. Again the physical symptoms of nerves were undeniable as he stood over the putt. Again he willed himself to concentrate on his putting process. The ball broke hard left to right and dove in. He pumped his fist again and moved through the roars to the tee at No. 17.

He was again eight under par for the day and he wanted another birdie. But No. 17 is a long par five, 578 yards, unreachable for Brad. That did not undermine his belief that he could make birdie. All he wanted to do was lay up to give himself a good wedge shot to the green, then trust his putter. He hit a fine wedge, but it caught the slope leading to the upper tier of the green, where the pin was. A foot or two farther and it might have been knocked stiff. But it rolled backwards, down the slope, and left him thirty feet away. That did not bother him. He believed that he could make the next putt, and he hit it beautifully. It stayed right on the edge of the hole. He could not believe it didn't fall. Days later, looking at the videotape, he still couldn't.

Standing on the tee at No. 18, he knew that whatever slim chance he had had to win the tournament was probably gone. He had no idea where he stood for the Ryder Cup team. He got under his drive for the first time that day, popped it up, and left himself twenty or thirty yards short of his accustomed spot in the eighteenth fairway. He tried to hit the same kind of hard 5-iron he'd hit at No. 1. He didn't catch it as well, and he wound up about five yards short of the green, looking at an uphill chip.

The eighteenth green at Riviera is in the middle of a natural grass amphitheater, and by now it was filled with people. There was an enormous scoreboard on the hillside, and Brad looked at it. He saw he was in fourth place. He still didn't know exactly what he needed to do to make the Ryder Cup team, but he knew it was extremely important to finish his round by remaining focused until his ball was in the hole.

He hit his chip a touch too hard. It rolled over the dry, crusty back half of the green and didn't stop until it was twelve feet past. Brad thereupon forgot about the Ryder Cup and the standings. He thought only of making his twelve-footer.

He read the green from both sides of the hole and noticed that there were three or four spike marks in his line, about two feet short of the hole. This time, he told himself that there was nothing he could do about them. He told himself to start the ball on its line and trust that it would hold that line as it got to the hole.

It did. The roar of the crowd reverberated around the amphitheater. It was the loudest sound Brad had ever heard on a golf course.

Brad had closed with a 63, the lowest final round score ever in a PGA Championship. No one has ever shot a better score in a major championship.

He made his way to the scorers' tent through a throng of screaming people and signed his scorecard. Someone from CBS invited him to climb up to the announcers' booth and talk about his round. And it was only there that he learned, from the CBS producers, that the Ryder Cup team was within his grasp.

A few minutes later, Davis Love III and Fred Couples called the locker room to let him know he had made it. That was typical of the way so many golfers, though remaining competitors, find ways to support and encourage their friends on the tour.

IF YOU'VE GOTTEN the impression that a great round of golf comprises dozens of skirmishes in the mind of the golfer, not all of which are won, you're right. I have recounted this round in detail because it illustrates that even the best players, playing as well as anyone has ever played, wage constant war with doubts and fears and distractions. Some weeks it's easier than others. But if they don't conquer the doubts on a particular shot, the best players pick themselves up and gather themselves to work on the next one. That's what Brad did in the final round of the PGA. He wasn't perfect; he was merely striving for perfection. He disciplined his mind to give himself the best chance he could to play as well as he could. And he saw how good that could be.

Of course, it doesn't always work out that well.

Thinking well can't guarantee shooting low scores or winning. It only gives a player the best possible chance to score well and win. If it were foolproof, golf would not be a game. It would be a laboratory experiment.

Fortunately, it's a game. Brad's results in the Ryder Cup demonstrated that.

The Ryder Cup is not, I think, as significant for a player as winning a major championship. At least, I've never had a player tell me he's dreamt for years about winning a singles match at the Ryder Cup. But I do often hear that players have been dreaming of winning the Masters or the U.S. Open since they were five years old.

The Ryder Cup is, however, a tremendous television spectacle, and it confronts its players with a unique set of mental challenges. First, of all, they're representing their countries rather than playing for themselves. If a player has an off-week in a regular tournament, he slams the trunk shut on Friday, goes home, and few people care except for his family and friends. He can try again next week. If he has a bad week at the Ryder Cup, all the golfers of two continents know and care about it. More important, he's let down his teammates, the peers whose opinions and esteem he values most highly. And there is no next week.

Brad and Davis invited me up to Oak Hill to watch them play in the 1995 matches, and we talked about the team aspects of the event. I reminded them of their days on college golf teams, Brad at Furman and Davis at North Carolina. They made their best contributions to their teams by taking care of themselves and their rounds. Once that was over, they could cheer and concern themselves with what the rest of the team was doing. They ought, I thought, to approach the Ryder Cup the same way. Take care of their own games, and then enjoy being part of the team.

But neither the team format nor the outside pressure affected the essence of the challenge. They had to do the same thing they have to do in every competitive round: stay in the present and commit themselves to their routines.

They both responded well. Davis split four matches over the first two days of foursomes and four-ball play. Brad split two. Davis won his singles match over Costantino Rocca, 3 and 2. Brad lost his to David Gilford, 1 down.

Brad tried to blame himself for the loss of the Cup, since he had a chance, by parring the eighteenth, to halve the match with Gilford and salvage half a point.

But I knew, and he knows, that he had nothing to blame himself for. He trusted his driver very well for the entire round on a very tough driving course. He putted well, burning the edge of the hole half a dozen times. But Gilford, who is supposed to be a better ball-striker than putter, putted better. He was one up going into the last hole.

On the eighteenth tee that Sunday afternoon, some very good players found they could not trust their swings and they hit ugly, awkward tee shots. Brad hit an excellent drive, long and in the fairway. Gilford was well behind him, and hit a 4-wood long and left of the green, behind the grandstand. Brad hit a 5-iron that perhaps caught a gust of wind and fell just short, in a bunker.

From his drop area, Gilford had no chance to pitch to the green and hold the ball on the putting surface; the ground was too hard. He tried to run the ball down to the green, but it got caught in the heavy rough. He was lying three.

Davis, who had finished his match, was in the crowd behind Brad, exhorting him. "Hole it, Fax!" he yelled.

Brad envisioned a low, running sand shot that would feed toward the hole. And he hit it, but just a smidge too hard. The ball stopped seven feet away.

Gilford then chipped poorly, stopping his ball about twelve feet below the hole.

Then Gilford sank his putt. He was down in five. Brad needed his putt to win the hole and halve the match.

It was no easy putt. It was going to break, and the amount it would break would depend on the speed. Brad needed to get both the speed and the break precisely right.

He read the putt and stepped up to it. He thought the right thoughts. He hit the ball well.

And it hung up on the high side of the hole.

That doesn't mean that Brad didn't play well, that he wasn't mentally tough and that he won't take some very positive memories from his Ryder Cup experience. It means that Oak Hill, set up as it was that day, was an extraordinarily difficult golf course. And golf is an extraordinarily difficult game. If you love golf as Brad does, you love the fact that it is this way.

All a player can do is stay in the present, commit himself to the process of hitting good shots, and give himself the best possible chance.

How Fred Arenstein Broke 80

....
....
....

PROFESSIONALS LIKE BRAD FAXON ARE BY NO MEANS THE ONLY GOLFERS who can benefit from paying full attention to the business at hand—staying in the present—and from an unwavering commitment to the process of hitting good shots. Both concepts are as beneficial for weekend golfers as they are for touring pros. A golfer I know named Fred Arenstein demonstrates why.

Fred is an accountant who lives in northern New Jersey. He started playing more than thirty years ago, when he was a kid in Albany, N.Y. In those days, the Albany municipal course would let a boy play unlimited golf, all summer long for twenty dollars.

The course became Fred's summer camp. He and his buddies used to hop on bicycles every summer morning, ride out to the course, and play eighteen holes. The back nine was hilly and long, and there were no motorized carts in those days. Consequently, older golfers stayed away in the heat and the boys had it almost to themselves. They would hang out there and play more holes each day.

As a boy, Fred never took a lesson. He generally hit a big

slice. Like a lot of players with flawed swings and a zest for competition, he developed a good short game to compensate for his errant long shots. He spent a lot of time around the practice green, chipping and putting.

As he got older and more serious about the game, Fred took a few lessons to straighten out his slice. He developed a technique in which he cocks his wrists early in the backswing, very deliberately setting the club on an inside-to-out path. When it's working, he hits a reasonably reliable high draw.

Though he's a burly guy, Fred doesn't hit the ball particularly long, and he doesn't even carry a driver. He tries to keep the ball in the fairway and around the green and relies on his chipping and pitching to bail him out of trouble. His handicap for years has ranged from 12 to 18, placing him in the broad middle of the golfing spectrum.

About ten years ago, he settled in New Jersey and started playing at Francis Byrne Golf Course. Byrne is a fine old public course, a former private club that was deeded to Essex County years ago. The sand in the bunkers can get a little muddy and the tees can be a little bald. But it's 6,653 yards from the back tees, and it's an honest test of golf.

Fred has a regular game there, on Saturday mornings, with his friends Larry Pinilis and Barry Forester. To get a Saturday tee time, at least one member of the group has to rise early Thursday morning and show up at the course well before dawn; the line starts forming at around 4 A.M.

But that's not such a hardship in the summer, because there's enough warmth and enough daylight to tee off at 6:30 A.M. and get in a round before work. Fred's boss doesn't mind if he comes in at 11 on Thursday mornings as long as he stays late to compensate.

That's Fred's summer golfing regimen: a round on Saturday, maybe a round on Thursday morning, some chipping and putting practice, and maybe a trip or two to a driving range in the evening.

Fred's game last summer was pretty consistently in the 80s. He'd shoot 86 or 85 most of the time. On a good day, he'd get into the low 80s. On a very good day, he might go out in 37 or 38 strokes. But invariably, when that happened, he'd balloon a little on the back side, bringing it home in 44 or 45 strokes. Once, he'd needed only a par four on the eighteenth hole to shoot 78. One of his partners mentioned it, and, unnerved, he made six.

That frustrated Fred. Like a lot of golfers, he saw 80 as the border that separates the kingdom of golfers from the kingdom of duffers. Mathematically, there's not much between 80 and 79; it's a difference of less than two percent. But in Fred's mind, and I suspect in the minds of hundreds of thousands of others, 80 seemed as big a barrier as the Atlantic Ocean did to pre-Columbian Europe.

It was, in fact, a mental barrier. Fred's swing and touch were sufficient to get him into the high 70s. But to do it, he had to refine his mental game.

In mid-season, he picked up a copy of *Golf Is Not a Game of Perfect*. I'm pleased to say that he found some ideas in the book that helped him. The first group of ideas concerned the process of hitting good shots.

First of all, he learned to play with whatever swing he brought to Francis Byrne on a given day. In his occasional practice sessions, Fred tended to be very analytical about his full swing. He thought about where his clubhead was, whether his swing plane was correct, and other mechanics.

Francis Byrne had no practice range, so Fred's first long shot of any day at the golf course was taken from the first tee. If it went awry, he typically fell into the same frame of mind he had at the driving range, trying to analyze and fix his swing.

This is one of the worst things a golfer can do. Not even

professionals who study and teach the swing for a living can consistently tell what went wrong in their own bad swings. Most of the key movements happen behind them, out of sight, so they can't see them.

Even a pro who's watching someone else swing, if he's honest, will admit that he can't diagnose swing flaws with certainty unless he can look at slow-motion videotape.

So how is a weekend player supposed to diagnose his own swing glitches?

He can't.

But most amateurs try to. They start thinking about how far they turn, or how their hips uncoil, or squaring the clubface as they bring it through the impact zone. And those kinds of thoughts tend to make a swing tense and arrhythmic.

Instead of trying to fix his swing, Fred started dropping down to a club he felt he could trust. If that meant hitting only 7-irons for a few holes, he hit only 7-irons, until he felt he was warmed up and ready for the longer clubs.

This is a very sensible approach for weekend players, but not many have the nerve to use it. I see so many amateurs who pull the driver out on every par four and every par five because they think that's what a man's supposed to hit. They play it, even though when it's time to swing they're scared to death of hitting it out of bounds. As a result, they often do hit it out of bounds. They'd be much better off playing a shorter club that they felt confident about and playing the course 150 yards at a time. Their scores would be lower.

Fred started to pick out specific targets for his shots. And he developed a pre-shot routine that he tried to employ before every stroke.

His process, then, involved trusting his swing, picking out a target, and repeating a routine.

All of those things helped him to focus his attention on the present, on the shot at hand. In fact, he came up with a thought that reinforced this good tendency.

Okay, Fred, he would say to himself. *Just make one more good shot, like it was the last shot you were going to hit.*

He had been a player who kept close track of his score, as an accountant might, adding up the numbers as he went along, multiplying and dividing. He was the type of player who knew that if he shot 28 for the first six holes and kept to that pace, he would have an 84.

That was the last aspect of his mental game he needed to change.

Nearly all golfers would be better off if they forgot about the score as they played.

Fred's breakthrough came in a casual round, just after dawn on a midsummer Thursday morning. Barry and Larry had come down to Francis Byrne to join him.

No. 1 at Francis Byrne is a good starting hole for a course with no practice range. It's a short par five, 456 yards from the white tees, with a flat, generous fairway and no water. It's a hole on which three decent shots will find the green and get the player started with a par.

But Fred started off badly. His tee shot at No. 1 was in trouble, and he made six, a bogey.

In the past, Fred had always figured that he needed a par at No. 1 to shoot a good round, particularly since No. 2 was one of the tougher holes on the course, a 211-yard par three guarded by a deep bunker on the left side.

But it's significant how wrong these kinds of assumptions often turn out to be. Players who make great scores often get their birdies on holes they consider very tough. They par the easy ones. And I've often seen a player shoot a good score after botching the first hole, because he lowers his expectations and relaxes.

Fred did the right thing at No. 2. He took out his 7-wood and picked out a target, a tree on a hilltop behind the green. He hit a great shot that rolled up onto the green about fifteen feet from the hole. He made the putt for a birdie.

That settled Fred down. He made fours on the next four holes. He knew that he was one over par as he stood on the tee at No. 7. He pulled his tee shot into the woods there and made bogey. That set him off on a string of bogeys that left him seven over par as he reached No. 13.

He didn't play No. 13 particularly well, either. His approach shot found a bunker. But he blasted out to within a foot of the hole and saved his par. That set off another string of fours that lasted the rest of the way in.

The string of bogeys in the middle of the round had proven to be a blessing, the last key to breaking 80. For after making a few of them, Fred forgot about the score. He stayed in the present and just tried to go through his routine on each shot. Throughout the back nine, he didn't know where he stood in relation to par or to 80.

He was pleasantly surprised when one of his buddies added up the numbers. He'd shot 78.

THERE'S A WIDESPREAD misimpression among weekend golfers that to shoot in the 70s, a player must have a swing that a pro could envy. It's not true.

On the average golf course, from the white tees, a lot of players could break 80 at least once in a while. All they need is a swing they can repeat with fair consistency, a good short game, and the right mental approach. Like Fred Arenstein, they need to stop keeping track of their scores and focus their attention exclusively on the present.

No. 3

How Jay Delsing Kept Trusting

NOT MANY OCCUPATIONS HAVE SANCTIONS AS FINAL AND AS DAUNTING as the cut that comes after thirty-six holes of every professional golf tournament. If I have a couple of bad days in the classroom, I can go back and try to do a better job the third day. But a golfer who isn't on his game for the first thirty-six holes has no such luxury. He gets no second chance and he earns no money. He can only tote up his lost expenses and get out of town. Miss a skein of cuts, and a sense of failure and foreboding can infest a golfer's mind the way termites infest a home—unwanted, hard to get rid of, and very destructive. Missing cuts can cause a golfer to start playing to not miss cuts, which is a sure way to miss more of them.

In the first few months of 1995, my friend Jay Delsing missed nine in a row.

I started working with Jay in 1990. He was a player with obvious talents. He'd been an outstanding junior golfer in St. Louis, where he grew up. He played on some excellent UCLA teams with players like Corey Pavin, Steve Pate, and Duffy Waldorf. Once in a while, on tour, he would burn up a golf course.

He's set or tied course records at a couple of PGA Tour stops with scores like 61 and 62. But in the first five years of his pro career, he hadn't been able to win a tournament, and he'd had to go back to qualifying school twice in order to stay on tour.

In those five lean years, Jay often fell victim to a confidence-debilitating syndrome that can destroy the careers of players who don't win soon after they join the tour.

He would generally arrive at a tour course on Monday and play a practice round. He'd practice again on Tuesday. And during those rounds he'd play well, shooting in the 60s.

But on Wednesday he couldn't play a practice round because Wednesday is pro-am day, and Jay wasn't ranked high enough to be invited to play in many pro-ams. Being diligent and ambitious, he would resolve to practice hard. He would go to the practice tee early and stay late. And that was a dangerous place for him to be.

Practice tees on the PGA Tour are crawling with people obsessed with the mechanics of the golf swing. Some are players. Some are teaching pros who want to make a name for themselves and offer unsolicited lessons. Some are even less qualified—equipment company representatives or fans. Hang around a tour practice tee for an hour or two and you're likely to hear a dozen theories about how to execute a particular portion of the golf swing, half of which conflict with the other half.

I certainly understand the importance of sound swing mechanics. But there is a time and place for working on mechanics, and it is not on the eve of a tournament. Lots of the players I work with have decided, at one time or another, that they need to improve their swings. The smart ones take some time off from the tour, go to a teacher they trust, and work on the new movements until they can execute them without thinking about them. Then and only then do they return to competition.

It's tough even for a successful player to shut out the buzz of swing tips and theories that is in the air on a tournament practice tee. Ben Hogan found a way to do it. He would go to the far right end of the practice tee and keep his back turned to the rest of the players. He didn't want to see how other people swung; he knew his swing was different from the norm of the day, and he didn't want anything undermining his belief in it. And he didn't want to discuss or debate swing mechanics as he practiced. But not many golfers have Hogan's discipline. They're gregarious people, and the practice tee is one place where they can loosen up and be friends with their fellow competitors.

It's even harder for a player who's been missing cuts to ignore the buzz. Missing cuts can undermine confidence. This is particularly true if the player doesn't have what is considered a classic swing and wasn't taught from childhood by a respected pro. Jay fell into that category. He started playing golf on a public course in St. Louis called North Shore Country Club. Then he picked up a few things caddying at a club called Norwood Hills. He learned a lot from his father, Jim Delsing, a former major league baseball player who carried a single-digit handicap but was not a teaching pro. Jay has a good swing and lots of athletic talent to back it up. But even though his ball goes to its target when he's playing confidently, Jay's is not a swing many people would point to and say "That's a beautiful golf swing."

Certainly, the people on the practice tee weren't saying that. More often than not, by the time the sun set on Wednesday, Jay would be trying to fix something in his mechanics. He would be thinking that his swing wasn't good enough to win on the tour. And in that frame of mind, he would go out on Thursday and shoot something ugly—a 75 or a 78. The next day, thinking that it barely mattered, he might relax and shoot a 66 and make the cut by a stroke or two. Or he might shoot another 78 and miss it. But he was not consistently scoring well.

So when Jay came to Charlottesville to work with me on his mental game, one of the first principles we discussed was one that applies to every player:

A golfer cannot score as well as possible if he is thinking about his swing mechanics as he plays.

Research in sports psychology is only beginning to reveal why this is so. The best I can say is that the human organism performs repetitive physical tasks best if the brain is not consciously trying to guide the process. It performs best when an individual focuses on a target or a goal and doesn't think about how to execute the movement.

Consider, for example, the bucking, stalling effort of a novice driver who is trying to learn how to handle a manual shift. The movements are not that complicated. You push the clutch pedal in, you shift the gear, you let the clutch pedal out. But because the novice driver is thinking intensely about how to perform each step, he has no rhythm, no grace. The car lurches down the road like a drunk bouncing off lamp posts. On the other hand, consider the experienced driver. On the road, he never thinks about how to change gears. He thinks about how fast he wants the car to go and in what direction. He changes gears smoothly, effortlessly, without even being consciously aware that he's doing it. It's the same way on the golf course.

A golfer has to train his swing on the practice tee, then trust it on the course.

This applies as much to professionals as it does to an amateur like Fred Arenstein.

Sometimes, amateur players will hear this and say that it sounds fine for a professional who has a flawless swing. But they don't think their swings are good enough to trust.

First of all, none of the great professionals has had a flawless swing. Nobody would teach Walter Hagen's lunge through the ball. Nobody would teach novices to regrip the club as Bobby Jones did at the top of his backswing. Nobody would teach the flying right elbow of Jack Nicklaus. And nobody would teach Lee Trevino's swing plane. But they all won championships trusting those swings, even taking pride in their idiosyncrasies.

I was walking in a gallery with a teaching pro not long ago, watching Fred Couples play a competitive round. "Fred Couples," the teacher said, "blows my mind."

He was vexed that Fred, with his seemingly simple, unanalytical approach to the game, was one of the top players in the world, while he, who understood the swing so well, was helping hackers straighten out their slices.

"What you have to understand," I replied, "is that university professors, who are really good at thinking analytically, got to write the definition of 'genius.' They chose to define a genius as someone who thinks as they do, who breaks things down to figure them out, who makes the simple complicated. That'll make you a genius in academia.

"But if you want to be a genius in sport, you must be able to make what some people think of as complex into something simple. Because simplicity works under pressure. It lets you have rhythm and feel.

"Fred's a lot more honest than you are," I said. "If you wanted to get better and play as well as he does, you'd first have to stop deceiving yourself."

He looked at me and said, "What?"

"You heard correctly," I said. "You keep pretending that every time you hit a golf ball that doesn't go where you wanted it to go, you can analyze why it didn't, and that you can correct it after you've analyzed it. That's not true. It doesn't work. It hasn't worked. Yet you keep right on doing it.

"If I asked you to get on the golf course and be like Fred, just hitting it to your target time after time, even if some shots miss, you might try it for a little while. But if it didn't work right, you'd want immediately to go back to your old way of analyzing and correcting, as if that worked.

"Fred, if he misses a shot, just shrugs and accepts the fact that he missed. He doesn't think it's a big deal, because he trusts his swing and doesn't think he'll miss again. He doesn't try to figure out what went wrong and correct it. And because he trusts, he misses much less often than you do."

It's true that few amateurs have swings like Fred Couples or Jay Delsing. A lot of them have serious swing flaws that will, uncorrected, prevent them from ever becoming scratch players. But a lot of people who play in the 90s have swings good enough to score in the 80s, if they would trust them. It's a matter of getting the best possible scores out of the swings they have —be they in the mid-60s, as in Jay Delsing's case, or in the mid-90s. To do that, they have to trust.

This means, on long shots, that they think about where they want the ball to go, not about keeping their heads down, or keeping the left arm straight, or pronating at the top of the backswing. On putts, pitches, and chips, it means thinking about getting the ball into the hole, not about keeping the putter blade on line.

I prefer that golfers play without swing thoughts. The ones who fully trust their swings can do that. But I know that lots of golfers have been playing with swing thoughts all their lives and feel naked without them. I tell such players that they can have one, and only one, swing thought per round. Any more than one and they are liable to bog their brains down in a welter of mechanical thinking.

Some swing thoughts are better than others. In general, the less mechanical, the better. Reminding yourself to have a nice, even tempo is a good swing thought. Thinking about keeping the clubhead behind the hands on the downswing is not.

Once Jay understood this, his consistency improved and he had several years where he comfortably kept his tour eligibility.

But trust is not a collectible, like a rare postage stamp, that you can buy, mount, and own forever with no additional effort. Every golfer needs to work on trust in every competitive round he plays.

And in Jay's case, there can be a fine line between trusting and being reckless. Jay is instinctively an aggressive player, with a talent for shaping iron shots. Sometimes, though, he would get too aggressive. He would go for sucker pins and pay the penalty if he missed. He might find himself in the woods after an errant drive, with 190 yards and a few acres of sand between him and the green. He might then try to carve a 5-iron under a branch, through the glade, and over the sand, when the wise play was to lay up and trust in his wedge and putter to salvage par.

We talked a lot about having a game plan and sticking to it. There is nothing wrong with hitting a 1-iron instead of a driver off the tee on certain holes, I would tell him. The important thing is to trust the swing you put on the 1-iron.

For a variety of reasons, Jay was not playing well when I saw him at the Kemper Open in June. We talked a lot about keeping his equilibrium. I reminded him that missing cuts had nothing to do with the kind of man he was. And it doesn't. The difference between missing a cut and making a check can be one bad bounce in thirty-six holes of play. A golfer in a slump has to keep that in mind.

Jay missed the cut at the Kemper, but I thought he was making progress. The proof came a few weeks later in Memphis, at the FedEx St. Jude Classic, his next tournament.

The Tournament Players Club at Southwind is one of the tour's new stadium courses, designed for tournament golf with high drama in mind. Water is in play on about half the holes, and disasters are nearly always possible. But so are birdies. All the par fives are reachable in two shots and the winning scores are low. Winners at Memphis average better than 16 under par.

Jay got off to a solid start with a 69, but that score wasn't low enough to give him any assurance he would make the cut. His Friday round began on the tenth hole, and as he teed off, he was trying to trust his swing and stay in the present. We've often talked about the importance of trying to play great golf on Fridays, rather than trying to make the cut, and that was what he wanted to do.

No. 10 is a 447-yard par four; he drove well and put his approach shot only ten feet from the hole. Putting downhill, he ran his first putt four feet by. He missed the second.

At this point, Jay faced a crisis. He could have reacted by blowing up. A lot of golfers do this. They let the results of the first hole or two determine their attitude for them. If the results are bad, they lose their confidence and play badly the rest of the day.

But a good player, faced with some bad results, remembers that he determines his attitude. It is not determined by what happens to him. It comes from within.

Jay reminded himself that he had done everything right, mentally, on No. 10. He had believed each of his first two putts would go in, and he'd stroked them that way. The fact that they didn't, he told himself, was just the sort of test that golf throws up periodically to make itself challenging. In that frame of mind, he got the bogey back and then some. He turned in 33 and then burned up his back nine, coming in with a 63. He easily made the cut, but he was five strokes back of the leader, Jim Gallagher, Jr.

It rained again the next day, and once again, Jay started at No. 10. He played another solid round, and he was a couple of strokes under par when he came to his last hole, the course's ninth, a 450-yard par four, dogleg right. A pond guards the left side of the green.

Jay drove badly and found himself behind a tree, two hundred yards from the green, with the last sixty of those yards over water. The pin was cut in the front of the green. But he had a good lie, and he thought that he could hook a 4-iron around the tree and over the pond and still make birdie, despite the bad drive. Then he caught himself.

Trusting your swing doesn't mean that you have a go at every high-risk shot presented in a round of golf. It means, rather, that you prefer the strategy that gives you a shot you know you can make. Taking those shots enhances trust. It's easy to make a bold decision and then, as the downswing starts, become doubting and tentative. It's hard to be trusting if you know there's a 50–50 chance your swing is going to send your ball into the water.

Jay took out a 9-iron, played out into the fairway, and then hit another 9-iron to about twelve feet. He made the putt for his par. He thought about how, earlier in his career, he might have tried the 100–1 shot and taken a six, and he left the course feeling very confident, though he was still six shots back. In his hotel room that night, he made a commitment to himself. Although he had barely made any money all year, he was going to play Sunday's round with his head exactly where it had to be on every shot. He was going to trust every swing. He was going to play without fear.

And he did. On No. 3, a par five, he exploded out of a greenside bunker and holed his shot for an eagle. He birdied the fifth and happened to glance at a leader board. He was, remarkably, still six shots off the lead. He told himself to forget about what Gallagher was doing and keep his mind focused on each shot as it came. He parred along until he got to the fourteenth, a long par three. There he reminded himself to trust every swing from that point forward. He stroked a forty-footer that broke about twelve feet over a hump in the green. It skipped its way over some spike marks and went in.

At No. 15, a 385-yard par four, he hit his approach about twelve feet past the hole. As soon as he walked onto the green and saw the putt, he was seized by the knowledge that it was going in. He caught the eye of Kathy, his wife, who was walking in the gallery. He winked at her. And then he drained the putt.

Jay drove well off No. 16, a par five. As he walked down the fairway to his ball, he saw another leader board, the first he had looked at in ten holes. Gallagher, he learned, had been coming back to the field. With his birdies at fourteen and fifteen, Jay was only one stroke off the pace.

He had 250 yards left to the hole, which would normally call for a 3-wood, but he knew he was filled with adrenaline, and a 1-iron felt right. He hit it hole high, but well left of the green, leaving himself a tricky lob shot over a sand bunker.

Before he set up for the shot, Jay said a silent prayer. *Oh Lord,* he thought, *let me stay in the present and keep having fun.*

Someone ought to needlepoint this prayer and put it on clubhead covers. He didn't ask for divine intervention to get the shot close. He didn't pray that he wouldn't chunk it into the sand. He asked for precisely the attitude he needed to give himself the best chance to make a good shot.

He reminded himself that he had worked for years to put himself in precisely this sort of situation—playing with a tournament on the line. Then he walked up, went through his preshot routine, focused on his target, and hit a lovely little lob that stopped six feet from the hole. Jay has great touch with his wedge when he's trusting his swing.

He sank the putt, and he was tied for the lead.

The TPC at Southwind closes with two long par fours. No. 17, 464 yards, has a creek running across the fairway and a green flanked by three traps. No. 18, 440 yards, is a dogleg left, with water hugging the entire left side of the fairway and a lot of sand on the right.

Jay's tee shot at No. 17 went left. He couldn't tell if it landed in the fairway or the rough, but it caught a mound and kicked farther left, then caromed off a golf cart being used by CBS television and came to rest under a bush. He had to punch the ball out short of the creek. He caught a bad lie and couldn't get his third shot close to the hole. He made bogey. He was one back.

Now came the test. Could he stop thinking about the bad breaks and bad stroke on No. 17? Could he continue to trust his swing? Many golfers, after hitting into trouble on the left off the tee at No. 17, would take a look at the trouble facing them on the left side of No. 18 and start thinking furiously about how to prevent another hook. Others might reach for an iron, because on No. 18, the creek that runs down the left side broadens to a pond about 250 yards out. Jay had ample reason to think about those things, because in his years of playing at Memphis, he had put a few sixes down for No. 18. Some thoughts of those past disasters flitted, unsolicited, into his mind.

But he refused to entertain them. He took out his driver and focused on his target, which was the corner of a distant greenside bunker and a tree trunk behind it. And he let the shot go without thinking of how, mechanically, he wanted to hit it. The ball soared out over the middle of the fairway. It hung in the air a long time before it came down and stopped about 290 yards out. Jay picked up his tee, quietly joyous. This, he realized, was the kind of moment he had been living for. As he walked down the fairway, lined on both sides with spectators, he had the curious sense that he was fifteen years old again, playing in a Missouri junior tournament, about to birdie the last hole and win. He hit a smooth little 8-iron to about eight feet.

On television, announcer Gary McCord was telling people that Jay was at a disadvantage, because he didn't have any recent memories of good finishes on the last hole. When Jay heard about that later on, he snorted. He had lots of good memories. He had made hundreds of eight-foot putts. He drew on them.

People sometimes tell me that they can't control which memories rise to the surface of their minds before they hit a shot. Sometimes they think about a drive they hit pure and long down the middle; sometimes they think about one they sliced out of bounds.

This is normal. But I tell them that people can choose to develop long memories for their good shots and short memories for mistakes. And they can certainly choose which memories to dwell on. They can use their memories to help, not hurt.

Jay was determined to dwell on the good memories. As soon as he marked his ball, he felt certain he knew how the putt would break. He knew he was going to make it. It felt almost as if he had already made it. He went through his routine, stepped up without delay, and hit the ball right where he wanted to.

The ball slid just below the cup on the left side. Jay fell to his knees in disbelief.

He tapped in for his par and then waited for Gallagher to finish. Gallagher stumbled at the eighteenth. He was on in three and had about a twenty-foot putt. His went in. That's how tournaments are decided.

But Jay knew better than to feel like a loser. He felt good about trusting himself throughout the final round. He knew he had done everything he could to win. He had won the battle with himself by trusting his swing down the stretch while in contention. A player who wins that internal battle knows how to win. He knows his game will hold up under pressure. He simply has to wait for the next opportunity.

Buoyed by that feeling, Jay went on to have an excellent second half of the 1995 season, winning almost a quarter of a million dollars. He remained hopeful that his turn would come.

I think it will.

No. 4

How Davis Love III

Got Back to the Masters

DAVIS LOVE, JR., HAD TWO OF THE SOFTEST HANDS I HAVE EVER SEEN on a golfer, and a temperament to match. I met Davis when we were both on the staff at *Golf Digest* schools. He was the first person I ever saw who looked like his hands got softer through impact when he hit a golf ball. After I got to know him, I started calling him the King of Smooth. I liked him very much.

He was, in some respects, a country boy from Arkansas. Shortly after we got to know one another, he invited me to his home. He wanted to show me some of the volumes in his library of golf books, the ones that showed how some of the great players of the past had approached the mental game. But the first thing that caught my eye was an old, yellowed newspaper clipping, framed and hanging on the wall.

It told how a teenager named Davis Love, Jr., had made it to the quarterfinals or semifinals of the U.S. Amateur. The reporter had observed that this qualified him for an invitation to play in the Masters, and he asked if Davis planned to go.

"I don't know," Davis replied. "Where they playing it this year?"

He went on to obtain an excellent background in the game. He played at the University of Texas for Harvey Penick, whom he revered. He worked hard at the game. Too hard, perhaps. Davis Love, Jr., was one of those players who put a lot of pressure on themselves.

He decided that what he really wanted to do was what Harvey Penick had done: teach. And he was a wonderful teacher— demanding, yet patient.

As we got to know one another, I heard more and more about his two sons, Mark and Davis III. Teaching them had been his priority since they were old enough to hold clubs. I heard stories about twilight rounds of golf. Davis would come home tired from a long day on the lesson tee and the boys would greet him at the door.

"C'mon, Dad, let's go golfing!"

So off he'd go, walking on his tired legs, because the boys wanted to walk. They'd play four holes. And the boys would want a soda. So into the clubhouse they'd trudge. Davis might suggest that they resume on the first hole again. But the boys would have none of it. So he'd walk back out to the fifth hole with them, and finish from there.

Not surprisingly, they grew up loving the game.

But it was Davis III who had the yen to become a professional, and as the years passed, the game got more serious for both father and son. Davis, Jr., taught his namesake a long, fluid swing of enormous power. And through long hours of drilling in the hot Georgia sun, Davis III developed into a golfer with the potential for greatness.

As a teenager, Davis III saw his father in a different light than I did. Davis, Jr., was a grinder, a man who believed, for example, that the way to make sure you didn't miss short putts was to practice them—four hundred from two feet and then four hundred from three feet and then four hundred from four feet. He had, of course, picked up some sound ideas from Harvey Penick about the mental game. Penick taught Davis to be patient and to play one stroke at a time. But Davis III's perception was that his father was intent on the mechanics of the stroke, and believed that the best players got where they were by practicing until their hands bled.

In my conversations with Davis, Jr., I saw a different side. He told me that he didn't think he'd gotten as much from his own ability as he might have if he had known better how to relax and take pressure off himself. And he wanted his son to be better at it.

So he would sit with me, long into the evening, and we would talk about the psychology of golf at the highest levels. My ideas were not the ones he'd grown up with. But intuitively, he said, they made sense.

In 1987, when Davis III had been out on the tour for a year, Davis, Jr., suggested that he see me, and we got together. The immediate problem was Davis III's short game. He had led the tour in driving distance his rookie year and ranked high in greens hit in regulation figures. So father and son concluded, quite reasonably, that he needed to learn to get the ball into the hole better.

Davis III had the requisite mechanical skills with the wedge and putter; Davis, Jr., had seen to that. But he didn't have a consistent routine. Sometimes he would look at the hole, bring his eyes back to the ball, and tense up, thinking about the mechanics of his stroke. That became clear when I asked him to talk out loud about what he was doing as he prepared to putt or chip.

Davis was a big basketball fan and a friend of Michael Jordan, who had attended the University of North Carolina at about the same time. So we talked about the way a good basketball player's head operates. He could see that Jordan didn't stop in the middle of a move to the basket to think carefully about mechanics. Jordan locked his eyes on the rim and let the ball go. I wanted Davis to react to his targets in the same way.

To help break his old habits, I asked him to try a new putting routine. At its core, any good routine has three elements: a last look at the target, bringing the eyes back to the ball, and the start of the swing. They should be performed rhythmically and sequentially, so there is no significant delay between bringing the eyes back to the ball and beginning the swing. I want the brain and nervous system reacting to that last look at the target. A lot of players' routines are flawed because they let mechanical thoughts, like taking the putter head back on a certain line, interfere with that reaction. So I suggested that Davis start taking the putter back as he brought his eyes to the ball.

Davis understood the concept, and he adopted the new routine. The next time I saw him, at the Byron Nelson Classic in Dallas, he felt relieved to be free of the old ways that had had him standing over the ball a long time and getting tight before he hit the putt. He felt, he told me, like he was just walking up to the ball and hitting it. It felt good, and he was hitting the putts solidly. He was "freeing it up." The new problem was that he was hitting too many putts six feet past the hole.

"What are you freeing it up *to?*" I asked.

"I'm not," Davis said. "I'm just looking at the hole and hitting it."

He was so into freeing it up that he forgot to free it up to something in particular. That was like a pitcher throwing freely toward the south end of the ballpark, instead of to the pocket of the catcher's glove. Davis had to focus on the tiniest possible target—on the line that would take the ball from its spot on the green to the back of the cup. He had to be thinking about its end point in the hole.

He had, in effect, gone from being too careful to being careless with his putts. Freeing it up to nothing is sloppy golf; it's too loose. Getting careful and trying to steer the ball is too tight. It's easy to fall into either habit. But they don't work.

In putting, the challenge is to make a free stroke to a specific target. Guiding, steering, or being careful with a putting stroke are faults bred by doubt.

Davis went back to the practice green. A week or two later, at the Colonial National Invitation in Fort Worth, it came to him. He started dropping putts from all over the golf course.

For Davis, the image that solidified the happy medium was an unusual one. He thought about one of those little executive desk toys that have a row of five stainless steel marbles suspended from strings. Set the marble on the left in motion and it swings back, hits the stationary marbles, and knocks the right-end marble into mirror-image motion. The right-end marble, in turn, swings back and starts the sequence in the opposite direction. A rhythm begins as they bounce off one another. Click-click-click. He said he felt that he replicated that rhythm as he looked at the hole, looked at the ball, and took the putter back.

Over the years since then, that rhythm has been the key to Davis's putting routine. Some people depart from their routines by getting too tight and careful; Davis tends to lose his touch by overemphasizing being loose and free and forgetting about the target. At the British Open in 1994, he found that he was swinging the putter well before he got his eyes back to the ball, rather than following that click-click-click rhythm that helps him lock into the target. But the memory of the rhythm helped him correct himself.

Davis and I worked on the same principles for his full swing routine. Again, his problem was that he tended to get a little careless. I asked him to make sure he took time to decide precisely what kind of shot he wanted to hit before he took his practice swing. Then he needed to make that swing serious, as if he were really hitting. When he does those things and looks at a specific target, he's a great striker of the ball.

We talked about practice regimens and preparing for tournament play. I'm not a believer in hitting hundreds of practice balls, especially putts, just for the sake of hitting them. I'm much more interested in the quality of a player's practice than the quantity. If one of my players walks onto the practice green, drains four ten-footers in succession, and knows that his routine is sound, I see no reason why he should stay on the green and keep putting just so he can say he hit his daily quota. He's only likely to miss some, tarnish his confidence, and get the urge to start working on his putting mechanics.

A player has to know himself. He has to know how much and what kinds of practice he needs to be at his best. And he has to put that practice in. But going past that point can be counterproductive. It's analogous to the twin pitfalls—being too tight or too sloppy—Davis had to learn to avoid in his putting routine. A player needs to find the happy medium.

This notion appealed to Davis. He has always wanted to be as good as he can be. He dreams of winning major championships and he is willing to work as hard as necessary to fulfill those dreams. But he wants to be his best as efficiently as possible. Partly because he's had wrist problems, he's not interested in practice for the sake of practice, not interested in the quantity of balls he hits. He has other interests that are important to him —his family and his hobbies. He loves to hunt and fish.

I told him that was fine. He could even use his hobbies to reinforce what we were striving for in his golf game. A fisherman who sees a spot in a stream and reflexively casts toward it has a lot in common with a golfer who sees a hole and putts to it.

But Davis also thought, erroneously in my opinion, that his father wouldn't have agreed. He remembers the taskmaster in his father, and he hears the whispers that he could be even better if he worked harder.

There is tragedy in this. Davis Love, Jr., died in a small-plane crash in 1988. Davis III felt the pain that any son feels at the loss of a father who loved him, and whom he loved. But he also felt, very keenly, the loss of a mentor. He often wonders about the conversations he and his father would have had. He's learned a lot about himself and about golf in the past seven years. He wishes he could chew over what he's learned with his father.

Based on my own conversations with Davis, Jr., I know several things. One is that he would be thrilled to see how much Davis III has accomplished. Another is that he would agree on the importance of his son's being relaxed and confident about his golf. He would, I think, say that Davis III is doing great and getting better. He would understand that his son might get tight, anxious, and worse if he started living and breathing golf twenty-four hours a day.

TIGHTNESS AND ANXIETY largely account, I think, for the problems that Davis used to have playing well in major championships. After he'd won on the tour half a dozen times, writers started including him on their perennial lists of "best players never to have won a major." Publicly, Davis always responded that since he had never contended in a major, it was impossible for anyone to say that he was capable of winning one. He was trying to reduce the pressure on himself, to lower everyone's expectations.

But privately, Davis's expectations were higher than any sportswriter's. He felt that major championships should be the easiest for him to win, because they're played on difficult golf courses. The difficulty of the courses, he reasoned, should eliminate the chance that an inferior ball-striker will get a hot putter and win. The majors, he thought, were made for a player like himself, a superior ball-striker who can also putt well. In particular, he saw himself winning the Masters. U.S. Open and PGA courses, which tend to have tight fairways and heavy rough, give an advantage to accurate hitters, even if they're not as long as other competitors. They would always be a tough challenge for him. But Augusta is made for long hitters. So his failure to contend there became a source of growing frustration. He didn't relax and play his best golf.

Going into the 1994 season, playing well in the majors was Davis's top priority. He arrived at Augusta thinking that he was playing well and putting well. But, as often happens when a player is too tight, he played badly. He missed the cut.

It hurt, and Davis went into a tailspin that lasted the rest of the summer. Golf stopped being fun for him. Worse, he stopped doing the things he needs to do to play well. At home, he practiced less. He'd fly to a tournament site on Tuesday, go to the practice range, and start trying to figure out where his swing was and what he needed to do to get ready. His native ability helped him get by, but after finishing second on the money list in 1992 and twelfth in 1993, he fell out of the top thirty and failed to win a tournament. At the time, he didn't realize what was happening. He thought he was the victim of some bad breaks and was very close to where he had been in 1992 and 1993. But he wasn't.

Davis started to come out of this funk at the President's Cup in the fall of 1994. Energized by the challenge of team competition, he got focused on his game again and played well. But it was too late to salvage the season. He missed the Tour Championship. He didn't qualify for the Masters.

I was only one of several people who told Davis that autumn that his commitment had slipped. So did Jack Lumpkin, Davis's swing teacher. So did Penta, his mother. And for that, Davis deserves some credit. Part of the trick of staying at the top in golf is surrounding yourself with people who are supportive, but who know how to tell you when you're off track. And part of the trick is listening to them. Davis did both.

Jack told Davis that he'd gotten a little careless with his setup and alignment; his swing had gotten a little too upright and loose at the top and too "handsy" at the bottom. I told him that he needed to stop thinking so much about winning major championships and commit himself to doing the best job he could of following his mental routine on every shot, from the first day of the first tournament to the last day of the year.

Starting in November and December of that year, Davis worked hard. This didn't mean he beat balls all day and wore himself out. But he did the work on his fundamental skills needed to lay a strong foundation for the next season. And he didn't return to the tour until he was confident that he had fixed his swing glitches and was mentally ready to play well.

He skipped a few of the early tournaments that he normally plays, in Hawaii and Tucson, and jumped in at Phoenix. It was clear he was much sharper than he had been in 1994.

But he no longer had the luxury of working his way back into peak form in relative anonymity. Because of his play in 1994, he had not qualified for a Masters invitation. The only way he was going to get one was by winning one of the first tournaments of the year. As the tour left California and reached Florida, this became a running sidebar for the golf press. Could Davis do it? The reporters pressed him at every stop.

He came close, finishing well at Phoenix, Pebble Beach, and Doral. The next-to-last chance came at the Players' Championship. With the TPC Stadium Course set up to be very difficult, he opened with a 73, then shot 67 and was tied for third. On Saturday, he shot 74, but he was still tied for fifth, three strokes back of Corey Pavin and Bernhard Langer. With the wind up, the greens dried out, and the rough high, he managed a 72 on Sunday. He was three strokes short of Lee Janzen's winning total. There was just one chance left, the Freeport McMoRan Classic at English Turn Golf Club in New Orleans.

The challenge of winning the one tournament he had left to qualify for the Masters was an extraordinary one. First of all, no one controls the outcome of a tournament. A player can only play his best; the rest depends on how others do. Second, no one can play his best if something deflects his attention from the process of hitting each shot well. The task Davis faced was like trying to perform brain surgery in the middle of a circus. The Masters was that distracting.

Moreover, he had to cope with the conflict between what he thought his father would have advised him to do and what his own experience told him was best. He thought that his father would have been on him to grind hard—to be on the range early Monday morning for a videotaped practice session, working on swing flaws; to fly to New Orleans Monday night, not wasting time traveling during the day; to play a practice round Tuesday morning and spend Tuesday afternoon on the practice tee and the putting green; to play in the pro-am Wednesday morning and then have another full afternoon of practice.

I suspect Davis, Jr., would in fact have had a different attitude. I think he knew that the grinding, practice-till-your-hands bleed attitude is great for a player who's trying to go from average to very good. But it's less effective for a player who's trying to go from very good to excellent. At the top levels of golf, the best players have an element of aristocratic nonchalance. They practice hard until they feel they're playing well. Then they know that it's time to ease off a little bit, to relax.

Davis, as he left the Players' Championship, felt he was in fact playing well. So he did what he and his wife, Robin, had planned to do. He drove home to Sea Island, Ga., with house guests—Fred Couples and his fiancée. He didn't touch a club on Monday. On Tuesday, Davis and Fred played a casual round on a new course Davis had helped to design, Ocean Forest. The range wasn't open yet, so they couldn't warm up or practice. Fred shot 68 and Davis 66. He and Fred flew to New Orleans and learned they'd been the only ones in the field able to play at all on Tuesday. It had rained in Louisiana, and it continued to. The pro-am was washed out on Wednesday. Davis had never played English Turn before. Now he would have to start learning the course in competition. He decided that he could figure the course out as he went along.

When the tournament started, Davis was still playing well. He opened with a 68, four off the lead. On Friday, his 69 moved him into a tie for third. And on Saturday he made two eagles and three birdies and shot 66 to take the lead.

Now Davis truly was like Odysseus sailing past the Sirens. As soon as he took the lead, the distractions intensified. People in the crowd were yelling, "Masters tickets! I need Masters tickets!" In the press room, reporters barraged him with questions. Did he think he could win and make the Masters? What would it mean to him to make the Masters? We had talked about these kinds of distractions in the past, and Davis knew what to do. Every time someone mentioned the Masters to him, he needed to think, *If I want to win this tournament and get in the Masters, I have to concentrate on my routine on every shot. I can't start thinking about the Masters.*

But it wasn't easy.

I called Davis at around that time. As frequently happens, we talked about college basketball. Part of my job is to find the most effective way to talk to an individual. A lot of athletes, including Davis, respond well to analogies drawn from other sports that they follow. In addition to Michael Jordan's shooter's mentality, I've often talked to Davis about Dean Smith. I'll point out that Dean, no matter what the other team does, has a plan that he executes. Davis needed to emulate that. And talking about basketball is a form of relaxation; I wanted Davis to relax.

Mike Heinen made a tremendous run at Davis that Sunday, shooting a 62. Just before he made the turn, Davis looked at a leader board and saw that he had fallen two strokes behind. As I've said, I don't recommend that players look at the boards. They're better off paying exclusive attention to a good game plan and a good routine; what others are doing can only be a distraction. But a lot of players can't or won't avoid the leader boards, and Davis is one of them. If that's the case, they had better be able to use the leader board as a cue to focus tightly on their own games, their own routines.

Davis did that. He was standing on the ninth green, waiting to try an eight-foot birdie putt, and he told himself, "O.K. Let's just play ten holes focused on routine. Just go through the routine and get freer every time."

Thinking that way, he knocked in the putt. The chase was on. He eagled the eleventh, birdied the twelfth and fifteenth, and regained the lead by two strokes.

At which point Davis listened to the song of the Sirens for a moment and nearly ran his boat on the rocks. His thinking moved from a tight concentration on the present, on his routine, to the future, to the allure of the Masters. He told himself, "All right, just par in and you go to Augusta."

He hooked his drive into a trap on No. 16, but managed to

reach the green and make his par. No. 17 is a par three, 207 yards, with water and a long bunker guarding the left side. Davis took a 6-iron and told himself, "Just put it somewhere in the middle of the green." He hooked it into the bunker, and though he hit a pretty good sand shot, he couldn't get up and down.

On No. 18, a watery, sandy par four of 471 yards, he aimed his drive at a letter in the "Freeport McMoRan" sign behind the green and blasted the ball more than 300 yards down the fairway, leaving himself no more than 150 yards to the hole. For him, this was a 9-iron. But then he thought, *No, I'll hit a smooth eight, just play it somewhere to the right side of the green. I've got the whole green to work with.* And he quit on the shot and pushed it into a bunker. Another bogey, and the tournament was tied.

Although Nos. 17 and 18 are tough finishing holes, a lot of armchair critics were doubtless thinking that Davis had choked, that he was afraid or lacked confidence.

Choking, though, is nothing more than being distracted by something. In Davis's case, focusing on the Masters had distracted him from two vital elements of his pre-shot routine. The first was picking out the smallest possible target.

A golfer's brain and nervous system perform best when they're focused on a small, precise target.

I like players to aim at something as small as a particular branch on a tree, not just a side of the fairway or the green. I like them to aim for a small spot in the cup or a particular blade of grass when they're putting.

When Davis aimed for vague targets like an area of the green on No. 17 and a side of the green on No. 18, he was setting himself up for trouble. As he told me afterwards, "The most dangerous thing you can do is hit a ball without knowing where it is going."

The second vital element he forgot was decisiveness. His first instinct told him to hit a 9-iron to the eighteenth green. Ninety-nine percent of the time a player will do better if he follows that first instinct and hits a decisive shot than he will if he reconsiders and goes to another club. Even if that second choice is technically the correct one, his swing is likely to be affected by doubt and indecision.

Fortunately, Davis had the self-awareness to figure out his mistake. He had never won a playoff before, but he knew what he had to fix to win this one.

He and Heinen each parred No. 16, the first playoff hole. They came again to No. 17. This time, Davis picked out a tiny target. He'd been drawing his irons that day, so he picked out a leg of the television tower behind the green, about fifteen feet right of the hole. He swung, and the shot took off, drawing toward the flag just as he had envisioned it. It nearly went in, but it stopped three feet away.

As Davis walked up to that seventeenth green, his face was red and twitching. Fans could see his lips moving. They could see he was talking to himself. It was a good thing they couldn't hear him, because the language was not pretty. He was berating himself for having forgotten about the small target and for his indecision on the seventy-first and seventy-second holes.

But he got over it in time to tap in the birdie putt and win the tournament. It was, I think, a turning point in his career. The next time we talked, he had things in the proper perspective. He was pleased and proud that he had reacted to the pressure of the last two bogeys and the playoff—not by getting upset but by correcting his error and getting back to his mental routine. He *should* have been pleased and proud.

•   •   •

BUT HIS SATISFACTION was unsullied for only an hour or so. The people at Augusta faxed their invitation to English Turn and let him know they were glad he'd be coming back to the Masters. His wife, Robin, planned a victory party. Jeff Sluman and Fred Couples called and offered to share the houses they'd rented in Augusta. Then, as he was leaving English Turn, someone broke the news that Harvey Penick had died.

The golf world knew what Harvey Penick had meant to Tom Kite and Ben Crenshaw. Not so many knew of his link to Davis. Harvey Penick had been Davis Love, Jr.'s college coach, but more than that, his ideal. "My Dad," Davis III would say, "basically thought Harvey Penick was the greatest man who ever lived. He *was* golf to my Dad."

Davis III had visited Mr. Penick several times. Each time, Harvey talked graciously with him and invited him to take an informal lesson. And each time, Davis III had the sense he was hearing again the things he had heard all his life from his father, only now from the original source. So when Harvey Penick died, it was, to Davis, as if another link to his father had gone with him.

He was no longer in a mood to celebrate. He didn't even want to follow his normal practice routine at Augusta. He wanted to fly to Austin Tuesday night, attend Harvey Penick's funeral on Wednesday, and fly back to Augusta just in time to hit a few practice balls Wednesday night.

Ben Crenshaw, ironically, talked him out of it. Ben had played with Davis on Thursday and Friday in New Orleans. And Ben had played badly. His toe was bothering him and he couldn't drive straight. His putting was so bad that he disgustedly putted the last three holes on Friday with his 1-iron. He missed the cut and went home to Austin, and he was there when Mr. Penick died.

On Monday night, Davis called Ben about the funeral. "Look, Davis," Ben said. "You've just won New Orleans. You're on a high and you need to be practicing and getting ready. We'll tell everyone you send your respects and you'll come out some other time to see Helen and Tinsley (Mr. Penick's wife and son)."

Davis was not convinced, but his wife and his mother both seconded Ben's advice. And, of course, there was a side of him that couldn't wait to get to Augusta. That side of him felt like a kid in bed on Christmas Eve, agog with the thought of the great things in store. It was not just that he could tell that his swing and his putting stroke were grooved. It was the way he had won in New Orleans—recovering his composure and coming back to win the playoff. He had proven something to himself.

In a sad, ironic way, his grief over Harvey Penick's death helped Davis. It eliminated any possibility that he would be euphoric or giddy after New Orleans. It helped him avoid the letdown that players often suffer the week after winning a tournament, when their thoughts tend to linger in the immediate past rather than focus on the present. It reminded him of many of the wise things that he had heard from both Mr. Penick and his father. Equally ironically, of course, grief similarly helped Ben Crenshaw to focus.

I spoke with Davis briefly before each round of the Masters. I tried to remind him to keep thinking the way he had in the New Orleans playoff—to let it go to a precise target, to follow his routine on every shot, to stay patient.

Davis was a little shaky in the first round, shooting 37 on the front nine. But it was a mark of his improved confidence that he did not get discouraged or impatient and turn that mediocre start into a round that would eliminate him from contention. He played the back nine in 32 and finished the day tied for ninth.

Another 69 on Friday left him tied for seventh. A 71 on Saturday gave him a 209 total, tied for eleventh with Greg Norman, but only three shots behind the fifty-four-hole leaders, Crenshaw and Brian Henninger.

He came to the course Sunday morning excited. When Davis is excited, he walks faster, he talks faster, he thinks faster. He has butterflies in his stomach and he is hungry, but he can't eat and he has a feeling akin to a runner's waiting at the starting line before an Olympic final. He is ready to go.

He knew that he had to find a way to slow himself down a little, to take deep breaths, to amble from place to place instead of striding. So he found a few old friends from home, got the appropriate passes and badges, and sat down with them on the front porch of the Augusta National clubhouse and had lunch. They talked about what they might do back at Sea Island after the tournament. Maybe it was that plantation atmosphere, that sense of leisure. Maybe it was the thought of fishing. Davis relaxed a little.

When lunch was over, he warmed up with Jack Lumpkin at the practice range, and then came over to the putting green, where I found him. I was thinking of something I'd heard recently about the UCLA basketball team. In the NCAA championship game, the Bruins had had to play without their great little point guard, Tyus Edney, who was injured. Despite Edney's absence, UCLA played a great game and won. Afterwards, one of the players credited their loose, confident attitude to something Ed O'Bannon had said to his teammates in a huddle early in the game. "Forget that it's the NCAA Championship," O'Bannon had said. "It's only a pickup game. Play street ball."

Davis and I had talked about something similar in the past. He knew how Michael Jordan liked to come back to Chapel Hill in the summertime and play in pickup games with other former

Carolina greats. Jordan always seemed to light it up in those games, even though the opposition was composed of all-Pro players. What made Jordan Jordan was that he would do exactly the same stuff the next spring, in the playoffs against the Knicks or the Lakers. Other, lesser, players would get the idea that playoff basketball was too serious to approach with the same attitude that worked in Chapel Hill in July. And that was one of the reasons that Jordan would dominate them.

So as Davis left the putting green and headed for the first tee, that was what I told him: "Remember, it's just a pickup game."

Davis and Norman, paired together, both parred No. 1 and birdied No. 2, a reachable par five. Davis birdied No. 5 and Norman birdied No. 6, sinking a putt from off the green. No. 7 became a key hole for Davis after he hit a bad drive into the trees on the right side of the hole. No. 7 is a short par four, only 360 yards, but the green and its surrounding bunkers and swales are treacherous. Davis had only 130 yards left, but no direct shot to the green. He had to hit a low fade under and around the trees, then over a deep bunker that fronts the green. He cut a 7-iron into the green and saved his par. Then he birdied No. 8, the second par five, and parred No. 9. He turned in 33. He and Norman were momentarily tied for the lead.

No cliché in golf is hoarier or truer than the maxim that the Masters begins on the back nine Sunday afternoon. Starting with Amen Corner, the course provides nine opportunities for drama, heroism, and disaster. The winner is usually the player who handles his game and his emotions best under this intense pressure.

"All right," Davis told himself. "You've got a challenge ahead of you. You've got a long way to go. Let's play the best nine holes you ever played. Get into the routine. Have some fun."

He hit two fine shots to within ten feet of the hole at No. 10.

Norman's approach was left of the green, down in a swale amid some pines. He looked like he would have to play well just to make bogey. But Norman bounced his chip off the slope and onto the green. It slammed into the pin and fell in. The crowd exploded. *Oh, gosh, here comes Norman,* Davis thought.

Routine saved him. Though he was transparently nervous and excited, he felt a kind of peace as he settled into the familiar chain of actions: reading the green, selecting the target and the line, aligning his body, taking one last look, and letting it go. Click-click-click. The ball rolled in.

He parred eleven and twelve, not easy holes to par in those circumstances. But No. 13, the 485-yard par five that is wrapped around Rae's Creek, has always been a difficult hole for Davis. His long tee shot always makes it possible to reach the green in two and make a birdie. But the second shot must always be hit from a sidehill lie that makes it impossible to hit his bread-and-butter approach shot, a high fade. He thought of the times he'd misplayed that shot; and he misplayed it again, hitting a 7-iron to the left of the green, way too far left, seemingly miles from the hole. He three-putted for a par that felt like a bogey. Norman birdied the hole, and now Davis was behind both him and Crenshaw.

He was, he would recall later, nervous. Very nervous. But over the last five holes, he forgot his mistake on No. 13. He learned how well he could play nervous.

At No. 14, he hit a wedge approach to two feet and made birdie. His drive on the 500-yard fifteenth was so long that he needed only a 9-iron for his second shot. It stopped ten feet from the pin, and he almost holed the eagle putt.

At No. 16, he hit a 6-iron almost exactly where he wanted it. It flew over the water and landed on the green, 190 yards away. The ball needed to be about two feet farther left. If it had been, it would have caught a slope and rolled down toward the pin, probably stopping within five feet. Instead, it hung on the upper terrace of the green, 60 feet away. Davis made a good run at the putt, but it was impossible to stop it close to the hole. He bogeyed it.

He told himself that he was not out of it, if he could birdie the last two holes. No. 17 is a 400-yard par four. For professionals, the drive past the Eisenhower Tree is not a problem. The approach shot is. Unless it's struck precisely, the ball can roll off to the left or right of the hole, leaving treacherous chips and making bogey a distinct possibility. Standing in the fairway after another long, straight drive, Davis thought briefly of some of the disastrous shots he had seen there. Then he reminded himself of all that he had learned that spring, of the discipline he had acquired. He said to himself, "Let's hole this shot," and focused tightly on the pin. He swung his wedge. The ball stopped six inches from the hole. He made the putt.

And, of course, he didn't win. He played the eighteenth bravely, getting up and down from the left side of the green for his par. He shot 66, and his total of 275 would have won sixteen of the previous eighteen Masters. But Crenshaw, playing behind him, was just as brave and a little better with the putter. Crenshaw won by a shot.

But Davis didn't lose. He had not only played his way into contention in a major championship for the first time in his career, he had played well down the stretch.

More important, he had learned a great deal about himself and his game during the ordeal of coming back from an off year and qualifying for the Masters. Those lessons carried him through some tough situations the rest of the season—he played very well at the U.S. Open and was one of the bulwarks of the American team in the Ryder Cup. He can only get better.

No. 5

How Val Skinner Won the Sprint

FEW PLACES ON A GOLF COURSE DEMAND BETTER THINKING FROM A golfer than the short, reachable, but dangerous par five. The eighteenth hole at the new LPGA International course in Daytona Beach is just such a hole—452 yards, with a lake lining the left side of the hole from tee to green.

When Val Skinner arrived there in the final round of the Sprint Championship last year, the need for clear, confident thinking could hardly have been more acute. Val had begun the day one stroke back of the third round leader, Kris Tschetter. A string of three birdies at Nos. 2, 3, and 4 had given her the lead, and she reached No. 18 ahead of Kris by two strokes.

Val, of course, wanted to win. She already had five wins on tour; she had her best year ever in 1994, capturing the Atlanta Women's Championship and more than $350,000. But from Atlanta through the first few months of 1995, she had experienced the frustration of playing well enough to win, but not winning.

And Val sometimes gets impatient when she doesn't win. She grew up in Nebraska, the daughter of a golf pro who put her first clubs in her hands when she was barely old enough to walk. She developed a very strong game. As a senior in high school, she won twenty titles. Her success continued in college. At Oklahoma State, she was the Big Eight female athlete of the year, twice led the nation in scoring average and was collegiate player of the year.

When she turned pro, she had to learn patience. No professional wins as often as Val had grown used to doing. After I started working with her, I noticed that she played best in the weeks when she could put her mind in a calm and quiet state.

But mellow serenity doesn't come naturally to Val. She's got an enthusiastic, outgoing personality, and she really loves the game of golf. She loves thinking about it and analyzing it. Combine those qualities with the frustration that seeps in when there's a long time between wins, and Val has a challenge. She has to work hard to cope with the high expectations she has of herself, to refrain from tinkering with her swing in competition, and to trust that adhering to her mental and physical routine will see her through to her best results. And she has to work hard to have the discipline to stick to her game plan.

Val is a long hitter. She averages about 240 yards off the tee, but she can crank her tee shots 270 yards under favorable conditions. Being a long hitter is an advantage, of course, but not an unalloyed one. Since she's long, she's frequently got a relatively short iron in her hands when she approaches a par four; she might have a 7-iron when the bulk of the field hits 5-irons. This increases the temptation to shoot for the pin. That's no problem when shooting for the pin is the smart play. But it can be disastrous when the pin is cut in a sucker position, next to a hazard.

Likewise, her length makes it feasible for her to try to reach a lot of par fives in two strokes. And in a lot of cases, this is exactly what she ought to do. You don't win many golf tournaments shooting even par. Most often, it takes something like 10 or 15 under. That means making birdies, and a reachable par five is the natural place for a long hitter to make them.

I don't teach any hard-and-fast rules for making decisions about strategy on par fives. But there are a couple of constants. First, a player must always weigh risks against rewards. What's the worst that can happen if a long second shot goes awry? If it can go out of bounds, with a stroke and distance penalty, that increases the risk side of the calculation. If a lateral water hazard is the worst penalty, the risk is reduced. A player could drop at the water's edge, pitch to the green and still make par if she sinks her putt. And if the worst hazard is sand or rough, the risk is minimal. In those cases, the potential for an eagle or birdie almost always outweighs the risk.

The second constant is the game plan. I want professionals to make their decisions about par fives on Tuesday and Wednesday, during practice. That way, their decisions are more likely to be coolly taken than they would be in the heat of competition. Of course, a plan has to have some flexibility, taking into account such things as the presence or absence of favoring winds. But in general, a player who thinks she is executing a plan is more likely to be decisive than a player who walks onto a tee wondering what to do. And decisive players, by and large, hit better golf shots.

Val, of course, had a game plan for LPGA International. And her plan called for playing No. 18 as a two-shot hole.

She had a lot of time to think about it on the tee. Play had slowed down ahead of the final threesome. The delay seemed interminable. Val had tried, during a previous delay, making small talk about the weather. But neither Kris nor Beth Daniel, the third member of the group, was in the mood for chit-chat.

So she noticed things. She noticed the crowd. She noticed

the television cameras. And she deliberately kept her eyes off the leader board.

Val generally doesn't want to know where she stands in a tournament. She has her game plan, which is designed to produce her lowest possible score. She wants to execute that plan. Any other information is extraneous and potentially distracting.

But there are a few situations where she wants to know. One of them is when she's standing on the tee of a hole like No. 18 on Sunday afternoon, in contention to win a tournament. She could tell, from the way Kris had played and the reactions of people in the crowd, that she had the lead. She didn't know by how much. She turned to her caddie.

"How're we doing?" she said.

"Great!" he replied.

"What do we need to do?"

"Par is fine."

That didn't settle her mind much.

There were, she thought, at least three clubs she might use off the tee: driver, 3-wood, and 3-iron. She'd been hitting the driver all week on this hole, playing the ball down the right side of the fairway. Twice, the strategy had worked and she'd reached the green in two. Once, she'd buried the ball in one of the fairway bunkers on the right side.

She thought about the shorter clubs. If she hit one of them, she'd have to hit a lay-up shot with an iron to the narrowest part of the fairway. That could easily leave her with a third shot to the green from a difficult lie in the rough. With the driver, she calculated, the worst that could happen would be a shot blocked right of the fairway traps. And if that happened, she could wedge back into the fairway and still have a short iron for her third shot.

So she went with the driver. As soon as she pulled the club

from the bag, she could detect a reaction. Peter Kostis, the television color man who was walking with the group, looked like he had just seen her pull out a ceremonial knife for hara-kiri. She could sense that she was flouting the conventional wisdom.

In this case, the conventional wisdom says that with a two-shot lead, you play safe with an iron off the tee, play for the easy par, and protect the lead.

In this case, the conventional wisdom was wrong.

I am a believer, and always have been, in a conservative strategy and a cocky swing. But the important half of that phrase is not the conservative strategy. It's the cocky swing. A conservative strategy is the means to an end. The end is a confident, decisive frame of mind as the golfer swings at the ball.

The right choice is the decisive choice.

And Val, following her game plan, made that choice.

Her mistake came in what happened next. As she drew the club back, the last thought that flashed through her mind was of the bunkers on the right-hand side of the fairway, the ones she'd plugged in earlier.

Keep it away from those bunkers, she thought.

Her brain and nervous system reacted to that thought. Her body stiffened on the downswing. Her hips held back and she yanked the ball left, into the water.

Afterwards, of course, all the sportswriters wanted to second-guess her. She'd flouted the conventional wisdom and hit it into the water. Second-guessing is their job. But they forget how often someone pulls out a 3-iron, gets conservative and careful with her swing, and pulls the ball into the water anyway.

Val walked off the eighteenth tee seething. But then she made an excellent decision, a champion's decision.

She decided that the only constructive thing for her to do was accept what had happened, put aside her anger, and go on from there.

Acceptance is critical after a bad shot. An angry player can't really execute a pre-shot mental routine.

A smart player knows that bad shots happen, often at the least convenient times. That's part of golf. The smart player accepts this, as Val did.

One of the ironies of the game is that bad players have a harder time accepting bad shots than good players do. Show me a foursome of once-a-month players who can't break 100, and the chances are I'll be able to show you a dozen instances per round of muffled curses, shouts of "I can't believe it!" and thrown clubs. And these are people who never practice and have swings that look like steam shovels falling off a ledge.

Winning professionals have much better grounds to get angry when they mishit a ball. After all, they've practiced for years. They have good swings. And their livelihoods are at stake. But if they're winners, they know better than to indulge in anger. They know that they're going to mishit some shots. They accept it when they do. They forget the bad shot and think about hitting the next one as well as possible.

Readers with long memories may be thinking right now, *Wait a minute. Didn't Tommy Bolt throw clubs into the water? And didn't he win the U.S. Open?*

Well, yes he did. But here's Bolt's considered opinion on the subject:

"Anger destroys both concentration and coordination, and that compounds both the strokes and the anger, and it's one helluva mess."

He was right. If high handicappers learned nothing else about the mental side of golf, they could improve just by learning to accept the result of any shot with equanimity. And they'd be more pleasant company.

• • •

FORTUNATELY, BY THE time she got to the edge of the water and took her drop, Val had put aside her anger. She walked along the edge of the lake, telling herself, "I am not going to let this tournament go. I am not going to give it away." And she drew on her reserves of strength and composure.

She had to, in effect, make a new plan for the hole. And the first thing the plan had to take into account was the lie she was facing. She had dropped the ball into thick rough, and because of the slope leading down to the water, the ball was well above her feet.

Had she remained angry, had she failed to accept her bad tee shot and put it behind her, Val could well have transformed a mistake into a disaster. The setup invited her to do just that. Thick Bermuda rough tends to grab the club's hosel and close its face as it comes through the ball. The sideslope tends to produce a flat inside-to-out swing. All the ingredients were there for an angry golfer to hit another hook into the water.

Val adjusted. She forgot about going for the green. It was too far away, particularly from that lie. She would have to plan to reach the green in two more strokes; she wanted her approach shot to be a full wedge. That meant that the next shot, her third, could be hit with a lofted club.

Too often, players who are in trouble on a hole fail to do this. They see that they're, say, 250 yards away from the green, and they pull out a fairway wood, though they can't hit the green. They're mad and they want to hit the ball as far as possible. But even if they hit the wood well, they'll leave themselves a half-wedge of some kind, which many players find troublesome. They'd be much better off in this situation hitting a 6-iron and a full wedge.

This is what Val decided to do. She didn't want her third stroke to put her in position to have to hit a little finesse shot with her wedge to the green. She could feel the tension affecting her body. She was aware of her own breathing; she could feel herself tightening up. She wanted to take only full swings in that state. So she pulled out a 6-iron.

Next, she adjusted for the lie. She took a stance that placed the ball closer to her right foot than she normally would. She opened the face of her 6-iron a little. She picked out a target, went through her routine, and hit a sound recovery shot, well clear of the water—in fact, into the rough on the right side.

This time she caught a good lie. She reminded herself that she'd hit this kind of wedge from the rough thousands of times before. And she hit a beauty, about five feet from the hole.

She strode to the green confidently. After Kris Tschetter missed her eagle putt, Val could have made six and still won. But she had no intention of making six. She lined up the putt and knocked it in for her par. She won in style.

After the victory ceremony, and after the press had grilled her, Val called me. She was wondering whether she made the right choice on the eighteenth tee.

"Maybe I should have just hit a 3-iron. Maybe I should have bunted it down the fairway," she said.

I told her that she and other great players with high expectations of themselves had to be careful to not let other peoples' criticism turn a victory into a defeat. I told her to remember that she had shown a winner's mind when she accepted the results of her tee shot and went on from there to par the hole. And I told her not to second-guess her club selection.

It's more important to be decisive than to be correct, I said. Because as far as I'm concerned, if you're decisive, you are correct.

No. 6

How Paul Runyan

Beat Sam Snead 8 and 7

WHEN THE FINALISTS IN THE 1938 PGA CHAMPIONSHIP AT SHAWNEE Country Club began making their way to the first tee, it would have been hard to find a spectator or sportswriter who didn't think the outcome was a foregone conclusion. One of them, dressed that year in a floppy newsboy's cap and a long-sleeved white shirt, was Sam Snead. The other, a natty wisp of a man with precisely combed blond hair, was Paul Runyan.

The seemingly essential difference between them had been apparent on the practice tee when they warmed up. Snead, then twenty-six, was in a couple of respects the John Daly of his day. He was a rawboned country boy, and he launched the ball. His tee shots regularly went 280 or 290 yards, gargantuan drives with the equipment of those times. Runyan, in contrast, looked Lilliputian. He was about five feet seven with his golf spikes on and weighed maybe 120 pounds right after breakfast. He would be giving Snead fifty or sixty yards off the tee.

And the golf course seemed to favor Snead. Shawnee was the first course designed by A.W. Tillinghast, the Philadelphian whose later work included some of America's classic championship layouts, among them Winged Foot and Baltusrol. It's hard to say now whether the Shawnee course was as good as those were. The band leader Fred Waring bought the place in 1943, added nine holes, and tore up a lot of Tillinghast's original design. But one aspect of the Shawnee course remains clear from old scorecards.

The course had relatively short par fives. Sam Snead could reach at least three and possibly all four of those greens in two shots. Paul Runyan, whose best drives traveled maybe 230 yards, couldn't reach any of them.

But there were a few other factors, a little more subtle, that gave Runyan a chance.

The first was the rough. Most of Shawnee's holes were on an island in the Delaware River. It had rich alluvial soil, and the rough grew thick and lush. A few years prior to the 1938 PGA, Runyan had played in a lesser event at Shawnee. He remembered that Bobby Cruickshank had found his ball in the rough, laid his bag down beside it, and then gone to help a competitor find his ball. A few moments later, he turned around—and couldn't find his bag. If a golf bag could briefly disappear in the Shawnee rough, there was going to be a premium on staying in the fairway. Runyan would do that.

The second—more important—factor in Runyan's favor was his short game.

From his earliest days in golf, Paul Runyan had understood the importance of chipping, pitching, and putting. He'd had to.

He was born in 1908, the son of a poor dairy farmer in Hot Springs, Arkansas. When he was a boy, the Hot Springs Country Club was founded not far from his family's farm. He began caddying there, though it was sometimes tough to persuade people that he was big enough to carry their bags. And he started to play whenever he could. He'd practice swinging in his father's pasture. He'd sneak into the club and play a couple of holes on the way to school. At recess, he'd take his one club and climb over the fence to the fifth hole and play that until the greenskeeper caught him.

On those occasions when the club permitted it, he would compete against the other caddies. He soon found that lots of caddies could outhit him. In self-defense, he began to focus on the shots where strength and size didn't matter, the short shots. He watched the members at Hot Springs and copied the putting technique of a man who believed that the hands had to be directly opposed to each other and the elbows bent, one directly behind the shaft and the other directly in front of it.

The same technique, Runyan found, served him well from off the green. Southern greens in those days were not green. They were made of oiled sand, because agronomists had yet to develop strains of Bermuda grass that could be shaved to putting length and still survive the summer heat. Oiled sand was inconsistent. Pitch to a soft spot and the ball would sit down and stop. Pitch to a hard spot, and it would take off, out of control. Runyan determined that it was best to hit low chips and get the ball rolling on the ground as soon as possible. To do that, he adapted his putting stroke and used it with his chipping clubs.

One day he played a match with two big, strong farm boys, the Lanoy brothers. On virtually every hole, they outdrove him. And on nearly every hole, Runyan would use his chipping and putting to get the ball in the hole before they could. When the Lanoys started snapping clubs over their knees in frustration, Runyan realized he was on to something. He had discovered that an athlete who wants to win badly enough will usually find a way. His way was the short game.

At the age of fourteen, he became the apprentice of James Norton, the pro at Hot Springs, and he learned the art of making clubs. Norton advised him to grow a mustache to make himself look a little older, and within a couple of years, Runyan began giving lessons; he is still giving them as this is written, seventy-one years later. In 1927, he got a big break. The Jewish community in Little Rock founded its own golf course, a nine-hole layout called the Concordia Country Club. Paul Runyan was hired as head professional. Membership was small, and the club was busy only on Wednesday afternoons and weekends.

This gave him the opportunity to practice, and he seized on it five or six hours a day. More than half of that time he spent on chips, putts, and short pitches. Nowadays, golf has more than enough statisticians charting rounds to demonstrate the importance of the short game. We know that in any round, the majority—as many as 70 percent—of all shots will be struck within one hundred yards of the hole. And we know that the wedges and the putter are the scoring clubs, that a pitch hit stiff to the pin or a long putt sunk saves a stroke, while a well-hit drive leaves a player with lots of work left to make his par. Anyone who fails to understand the importance of the short game today has only himself to blame.

But when Paul Runyan fell in love with his wedges and his putter, he was pioneering. He intuitively understood their importance in a day when relatively few players did. And he honed his short game to a new standard. From around the green, he started thinking not just about getting his chips close, but about holing them. He very often did hole them. By the time he began playing in professional tournaments, he was good enough to average less than two strokes into the hole from around the green. In other words, he holed out his chip more often than he took three strokes to get down. He calculated that in a seventy-two-hole stroke play event, if he could stay within ten shots of a long hitter like Snead from the tee to the green area, he could win. He figured he was at least ten strokes better within fifty yards of the hole.

That gave him a confidence that infused his whole game. If a player thinks that he can get up and down from anywhere around the green, he can relax and swing confidently on his approach shots. He won't be tempted to overswing at his tee shots. All facets of his game improve.

Any player I work with will testify that these are the same principles I teach today. Golf was and is a game where winners have to have excellent short games. If anything, the short game is more important today than it was sixty years ago, because the depth of competition is greater now than it was then and everyone can drive the ball pretty well.

I want players to fall in love with the short game as Paul Runyan did, to devote at least half their practice time to it, and to delight in their ability to use the wedge and the putter to defeat and confound players who are, ostensibly, better ball-strikers. I want them, as they go through their routines for short shots, to think about the hole as their target.

That holds true, and then some, for the average amateur. If someone brought me a group of randomly selected 25-handicappers, took us to a golf course, and told me I had a week to get all their handicaps under 20, I would first confiscate all their woods and long irons and lock them in the bag room. Then we would spend the week practicing chips, putts, and pitches. We'd play competitive games around the practice green. I wouldn't care whether they used Paul Runyan's chipping technique or one of the more standard methods. Around the green, whatever works, works.

I would teach these amateurs the same concepts I teach the pros, with one exception. A professional's threshold distance for trying to hole a shot ought to be about 120 yards. From 120 yards and in, a professional playing from a decent lie generally has to be able to shoot at any pin, even if it's cut close to a hazard. If he can't, he ought to consider another line of work. For the amateur, the threshold distance for using the hole as a target may be somewhat less—sixty yards, or forty. And there may be instances where prudence will tell the 25-handicapper that wedging the ball onto the green will have to suffice. Suppose, for instance, that he's facing a delicate little pitch over a yawning bunker to a hole cut only a few yards on the other side of the lip of the trap. He'll still have a small target, but it might not be the hole. It might be a spot closer to the center of the green, assuring that the shot clears the bunker.

But I suspect my imaginary class of 25-handicappers would be amazed at how often they would chip and pitch with the hole as their target and at how many strokes they would start to save by doing so—and by practicing.

There are, unfortunately, golfers who don't want to hear this. They want to believe that golf is about hitting the longest tee shots or learning to have a reliable draw on the 4-iron. They rebel against this fact of life:

As long as the rules reward getting a ball in a hole in the fewest strokes, golf will be about playing well with the wedges and the putter.

Such types existed in Paul Runyan's heyday as well. In 1933, Gene Sarazen and some other touring pros decided that there was entirely too much emphasis on the short game, particularly putting. They wanted to redesign golf to favor "shotmaking." So they prevailed on the organizers of some winter tournaments in Florida to expand the diameter of the hole from 4¼ inches to 8 inches.

The first tournament conducted with the big hole was called the Florida Year-Round Open. Most players began charging every putt. It didn't work. Sarazen had several three-putt greens. Runyan had no three-putts. He played his normal game on the greens, and he won by 11 strokes.

The advocates of the big hole decided this must have been an aberration. They staged another big-hole tournament, this one in Tampa, at match play. The finalists were Paul Runyan and Willie McFarlane, who was also a great short-game player. Runyan won again.

The experiment with the big hole ended abruptly that day. It proved only that there is no getting around the importance of the short game.

Snead and Runyan proved it again on the third hole of their match at Shawnee. They halved the first two holes, both with par fours. No. 3, a 458-yard par five, was supposed to be the first hole where Snead's superiority would show. It ran along the edge of the island, bounded by a strip of thick underbrush on the left side and guarded all around by rough. Runyan hit a driver and a brassie and was still short of the green. Snead hit a driver and an iron, but he pulled the approach slightly and failed to hold the green. Runyan pitched from the fairway and got his ball close to the pin. Snead, from the thick rough, couldn't get close with his shot, although it was shorter. He missed his birdie putt. Runyan made his. Snead was one down.

It may have helped that Runyan believed in a theory of match-play psychology that gave an advantage to the competitor "playing the odd." Under this theory, the important thing was to be the first to hit onto a green—the third, or "odd" shot played by a twosome on a standard par four. The idea was that by sticking the ball close, you could put more pressure on your opponent, especially if the opponent had begun to think complacently that he was going to win the hole because his tee shot was longer.

Walter Hagen, Runyan recalls, believed devoutly in this theory and had even developed some wily ways to use it. On a short par four, for instance, Hagen might use a tee shot that was analogous to a baseball pitcher's change-up. He'd take what looked like a full swing, but he wouldn't hit the ball very hard, ensuring that he'd have the shorter drive and would be first to hit his second shot. Then he'd stick the approach close to the pin. The opponent, startled by this seeming reversal of fortune, would then get so tense over his own approach that he was liable to botch a shot he might otherwise have executed easily. Or so the theory went.

I'm not sure how effective this kind of gamesmanship would be today. Touring pros rarely have match-play events anymore, and when they do, I advise them to play their normal games.

But I know that Paul Runyan thought that Snead's superior length off the tee made him vulnerable to the psychology of "playing the odd." That's the right kind of attitude to have. His alternative was to buy into the conventional wisdom that Snead's length gave Snead a huge advantage. If he had thought that way, he would have walked off every tee silently bemoaning his fate. He would have played worse. Winners find ways to think about the strong parts of their game and to believe that those assets will prevail.

If there were any lingering doubts in either player's mind about the power of the short game, the fifth hole erased them. No. 5 at Shawnee was called the Punchbowl Hole, a 108-yard par three to a slightly concave green. Snead put his tee shot inside Runyan's, which missed the green. Runyan chipped to about two-and-a-half feet. Snead's birdie putt slid about a foot past the hole and stopped directly between the hole and Runyan's ball. Runyan was stymied.

Under the rules at that time, players didn't necessarily mark their balls on the green to make way for someone putting from farther away. If the balls were within eleven inches of one another, or if either ball was within eleven inches of the hole, the closer ball was marked and removed. Scorecards of the time had an eleven-inch stripe on them called a stymie measure to gauge the distance. But if the stymie measure didn't save him, the player whose ball was away was out of luck. He had to play next. Sometimes, he might have a breaking putt that would give him a way to play around the closer ball. But quite often the hole was lost because of the stymie. This seemed unfair to a lot of people, and the rule was changed a few years later.

But that was the situation Runyan faced. Distances were measured. Snead's ball was fifteen inches from the hole, and Runyan's ball was thirteen inches behind it. Both putts were flat and straight. It looked like Snead would win the hole and square the match.

Runyan had no choice. He took his 9-iron and chipped for the hole. His ball hopped neatly over Snead's, rolled forward, caught the edge of the cup, and plopped in. In an instant, a hole that Snead thought was his had been snatched away and halved. Runyan got his ball out of the hole. Then he nonchalantly picked Snead's up and flipped it to him, conceding the putt.

"I have no idea what that did to Snead psychologically," he recalled recently. "But it certainly didn't help him."

Indeed not. Slowly, the thirty-six-hole match became a rout. Runyan took the greatest satisfaction from the results of the par-five holes. Of the seven that he and Snead played, Runyan won three, each with birdies, and halved the rest with pars. He went eight holes up with a birdie on the 472-yard par-five tenth in the afternoon round. The match ended when both players parred the next hole and Runyan had an insurmountable lead, eight up with seven to play.

"I saw it," Snead said at the presentation ceremony, "but I don't believe it."

He should have believed it. The importance of the short game should be engraved on the mind of every golfer.

FORTUNATELY FOR ME, Paul Runyan always considered himself first and foremost a teacher of golf. Nearly half a century after his triumph over Snead, he was still teaching at *Golf Digest* schools, which is where I got to know him and started to learn from him.

He remains a model for any golfer. At eighty-seven, he is spry and active. He gives lessons at a course near his home in California. And he still plays. He shot a 73 in one round with his friends recently—a 73, he added, that was not helped by a single long putt. He had a five-dollar bet with one of his friends that he would break 70 at least once before the end of the year.

He's still working on his short game. Paul tells me that he recently decided that the overlapping chipping grip he'd been using for about sixty years wasn't necessarily the best way to equalize the grip pressure from each hand. It put four fingers of one hand on the shaft against only three from the other. So he went to an eight-finger grip, which he reports gives him a firmer stroke. I can't wait to find out what innovations he comes up with when he's in his nineties. Such is his zest for golf and for life.

I hope I can be like him when I grow up.

How Patsy Price Broke 90

PAUL RUNYAN'S INTUITIVE UNDERSTANDING OF THE IMPORTANCE OF THE short game goes double for people with handicaps over 20.

If a good player like Runyan, who hit a lot of greens in regulation, figured that his short game could make up ten strokes per tournament against players like Sam Snead and Byron Nelson, how much would a good short game be worth to golfers who shoot in the 90s?

Enough, in most cases, to make them players who shoot in the 80s.

The statistics are simple. A player who shoots in the 90s generally hits no more than one or two greens per round in regulation figures. That means that on sixteen or seventeen holes, he or she is going to face a chip or a pitch to the green.

Most high handicappers, by definition, rarely get up and down; sometimes they take four strokes, because they leave a shot in a bunker or stub a chip. If they learned to get up and down even a third of the time, they would save enough strokes every round to play in the 80s at least part of the time.

And improving the short game doesn't require any complicated swing changes. All it usually takes is a few fundamentals, the right attitude, and regular practice.

I've seen this proven by a lot of golfers. One of the most recent was Patsy Price, a Californian who got in touch via the Internet after she read *Golf Is Not a Game of Perfect*.

Patsy took up golf as an adult, when she started dating her husband, Dave, a golfer with a seven handicap. One of their first dates was at a driving range.

Patsy knows what she wants. When she saw Dave walking to the tee with a bucket of balls, she asked him, "Where's my bucket?" And he went back and got her one.

He gave her a 5-iron and she started to swing. From that bucket, she hit one perfect shot. And that was enough to hook her.

Patsy had always been an athlete, specializing in softball. In golf, she found a sport where even a person of her size—she stands two inches over five feet—could propel a ball almost out of sight. That struck a deep chord within her.

Patsy is an engineer by profession, and she approached learning the game as an engineer might. She wanted to know the mechanics of the golf swing—where the leverage and the power came from. She wanted to smack the ball.

This is not a bad attitude for a beginner. Studies have shown that it's a mistake to teach a beginner to strive for accuracy in most sports. It's better to strive for speed. But, typically, little girls are taught to throw for accuracy. Little boys are taught to throw hard. That's where the expression "throws like a girl" originates.

Later on in an athlete's development, it's possible to teach someone who's learned to throw hard, or swing hard, to perform with more control. But it's nearly impossible to teach speed once the pupil has learned to throw or swing for control.

Patsy, fortunately, had no patience with teachers who patronized her and told her to think of simple things like rhythm and concepts like "open the gate, shut the gate." She especially disliked teachers who didn't take her seriously because she is a woman.

She kept looking until she found teachers who responded when she asked them to describe in detail things like the action of the wrists through the hitting zone. Her present teacher uses videotapes and computers to analyze his pupils' swings in minute detail.

And Patsy worked assiduously at her game. She developed a strong, fluid swing and she learned to hit the ball a long way off the tee—as long as a lot of women professionals. Within a couple of years, she was shooting in the 90s.

She and Dave got married and established a golf-oriented household. They have a putting green and a practice net in their living room to keep the muscles loose during the winter.

Patsy had big dreams for a golfer who started after her thirtieth birthday. She wanted to have a single-digit handicap. She wanted to play in the California State Amateur.

Her progress halted a few years ago, when she had a baby. For three years, she stopped playing. When she started again, she found she still had a few bad habits she'd picked up during her pregnancy. She tended to cast the club and hit a slice.

She went to work again on her swing, but her scoring didn't improve with practice the way it had when she first took up the game. She hit a plateau when her handicap reached 20, and for a long, frustrating time, she couldn't get past it.

A large part of the reason was Patsy's determination to improve her swing so that she could compete on a high level. It's great to have long-range goals and a commitment to work toward them. It's great to try to develop a better swing.

But sometimes, golfers forget that the object of the game is not to have a great swing, but to put the ball into the hole.

In competition, how you score is more important than how you swing. And Patsy tended to neglect work with the scoring clubs, particularly her wedges. She loved hitting tee shots—that was a problem in mechanics. She loved putting—that was an intellectual exercise that challenged her. She didn't bring the same intensity to her short game.

A round that she played on her birthday last year showed how much her scoring could improve if she did. To celebrate the occasion, Dave took her to a resort called Tan-Tar-A, in the Ozark Mountains. It has a tough Pete Dye course called the Oaks.

On the day they arrived, Dave and Patsy had time for nine holes. They played from the blue tees, which is something Patsy often does. She likes to compete with men, and she thinks she sees the whole golf course from the back tees.

She shot 50 for the nine holes.

The next day, she and Dave were paired with another couple. Patsy and the woman partner played the yellow tees, typically the senior men's tees. She shot a typical round: 50–45 for a total of 95.

That afternoon, she persuaded Dave to play again. This time, she played the red, forward tees. At the end of nine holes, she asked Dave what she had.

"Fifty," he told her.

As it turned out, he'd made a calculation error. She had actually shot 47.

But Patsy was livid. As far as she knew, she'd shot 50 for the front nine from the back tees; 50 from the yellow tees and 50 from the red tees, even though the nine played about 500 yards shorter from the red tees than it did from the blues.

It dawned on her that something she'd recently read in *Golf Is Not a Game of Perfect* was true. Scoring didn't depend much on how far the ball went off the tee. It depended a great deal on how well she hit the ball from within one hundred yards of the hole. And in that range, she had been playing sloppy golf.

She resolved to try some of the things I'd recommended. She focused tightly on getting the ball into the hole from around the green. "If I missed the green," she told me later, "I looked at that flagstick and I thought to myself, *this chip's going down.*"

When she putted, she thought the same way. Patsy had believed that anytime she putted from more than forty feet, she was in three-putt territory. She started thinking about holing her long putts instead of trying to get them in the general vicinity of the cup.

It helped, by the way, that when Patsy plays with Dave, he keeps score. When she plays by herself or with others, she keeps her own score, and she treats the card like an engineering data base. She keeps track of strokes taken, greens in regulation, length of first putt, etc. With Dave keeping score, she stopped counting all those things.

It also helped that she thought she'd shot 50 for the front nine and therefore had no realistic chance to break 90. She forgot about the score and simply played, focusing on each shot as it came, particularly the short ones.

She toured the back side in 39 strokes. When she reviewed the card and corrected the addition for the front nine, she realized she had not only broken 90, she had shattered it. She'd shot 86.

Just to prove it was no fluke, she shot an 86 the next morning.

Not every golfer, of course, will see the immediate benefits Patsy did when she changed her attitude toward the short game. Improvement is rarely so dramatic.

But if a person with a 20 handicap like Patsy's came to me and asked for just one tip to lower her scores, I'd tell her to do what Patsy did—to get enthused about that short game. Falling in love with the short game and playing golf confidently are intimately linked.

No. 8

....

How Tim Simpson Battled the Yips

....
....
....

A LOT OF GOLFERS HAVE TOLD ME THAT THEY HAVE THE YIPS, THAT putative disease that turns strong men jelly-kneed in the face of four-foot putts. There have been so many that sometimes I think you could staff all the pro shops around the country with players who mastered the art of striking the golf ball well enough to go on tour but could never get over their fear of putting. And of all the golfers I've tried to help with putting woes, none has fought the battle more tenaciously than Tim Simpson.

Tim's is a story of triumph and tragedy that's still being written.

As a boy, Tim was a good putter. He'd taken up the game when he was seven years old; his father gave him a putter to play with. He set records in high school and college. He grew up into a stocky bear of a country boy, and he made it to the tour at the age of twenty-one. He practiced his short game diligently. In rain, sleet, and snow. It didn't matter. He believed he could be the best player in the world, and he set out to do it. He was not afraid of winning.

But at some point, he started to lose confidence in his putting.

Tim can pinpoint the moment when his putting problem seemed to crystallize. It was in the final round of the Players' Championship in the spring of 1978, his second year on the tour. A gale was blowing off the Atlantic that day, with gusts strong enough to knock over a big tour golf bag. Tim had a one-foot putt on the seventeenth hole. The wind blew him off balance as he stroked the putt, and he missed.

The missed putt preyed on Tim's mind. It cost him several thousand dollars at a time when he was struggling to establish himself as a professional. It reinforced a notion that he had begun to develop that his putting wasn't tour quality. He fell into a spiral of bad thinking and bad putting habits.

Tim always thought of himself as a grinder. The code he was raised by held that you overcame your problems with hard work and determination. He started to spend long hours on the practice green. He was always one of the first to arrive at a tournament course on Monday.

He decided he needed to perfect his putting stroke. First, he concluded that the wind had affected him because he'd been standing up too straight. Tim is a very sturdy player, but he began to crouch over his putts more.

The leading money winner on the tour in those years was Tom Watson. Tim had heard that Watson, like Bobby Jones, advocated a short putting stroke, like driving a tack into the back of the ball. Tim had always been a putter who moved the club with his shoulders and had a long, smooth stroke. But in those days, copying Tom Watson's putting style didn't seem as self-evidently dangerous as it might seem now. Tim tried to change, to be more like Watson.

His search for the perfect mechanics prompted him to get tighter and more careful on the green. He started to feel very shaky, very uncomfortable—anything but the way an athlete should feel before he does something. That led to more missed putts.

And given the time and emotion he was investing in his putting, Tim's tolerance for missed putts dramatically diminished. He started to get angry just about anytime he missed a birdie putt under fifteen feet. Putting became almost a life-and-death battle for Tim. He walked around the course telling himself he simply had to make this, had to make that, couldn't afford to miss this. So every time he did miss, his frustration and anger grew.

The irony was that Tim's ability from tee-to-green remained constant or even improved. His confidence with all the clubs in the bag except his putter remained high. Tim became a player who could boldly thread a 3-iron between bunkers and over water to within a few feet of a dangerous pin position. Then he'd let the short birdie putt scare him.

The archetypal Tim Simpson hole, in his mind, became a long par four. He'd crack a tight, controlled draw down the middle about 280 yards. His opponent would be in the trees right. The opponent would be short and left with his second. Tim would draw a 7-iron in around four feet from the hole. The other guy would wedge onto the green to about thirty feet and make the putt. Tim would miss his four-footer. They'd both have pars for the hole, and Tim would be muttering to himself that somehow the scores weren't fair.

His putting, in short, was threatening to ruin him. It ate at him. It looked as if it might thwart his quest to realize his dreams. Some weeks were better than others, but he never felt confident that his putter wouldn't betray him. It was like trying to stay in a marriage with an unfaithful spouse. He couldn't relax.

He tried most of the putting cures that float around the locker rooms and practice greens of the tour like the magic elixirs they used to sell at county fairs. He fiddled with his setup. He fiddled with his stroke. He thought about keeping his head still. He thought about accelerating the putter blade through the ball. He thought about holding his follow-through.

Tim talked to Jack Nicklaus, who told him that he always stood over the ball until he knew it was going in. Then and only then did Jack start the blade back. But that didn't help Tim much, because Tim had always putted best when he took little or no time over the ball, when he just looked at the target and hit it.

He started to suspect that the problem was in his mind, and he went to see a psychiatrist. He did the Rorschach tests. The psychiatrist said he was perfectly normal.

But he was feeling lost and discouraged. In 1983, his friend Carol Mann of the LPGA Tour suggested that Tim might get some help from me, and we started to work together.

ONE OF THE first things I told Tim was this:

The disease called the yips doesn't exist, except in the mind.

For one thing, the yips are supposedly a condition of the nerves brought on by aging. Tim's problems had begun when he was twenty-two years old, so old age had nothing to do with them.

For another, research has failed to find any scientific, neurological basis for the proposition that age robs us of any of the physical abilities involved in putting.

But there are lots of golfers who either never had or somehow lost the right attitude about putting. They prefer to believe that they have the yips. Tim was certainly one of those.

I told him that he wasn't as bad a putter as he thought he was.

No one who gets to the PGA Tour and stays there is a bad putter. Some are better than others, but no one is bad. Putting is just too important a component in a golf score.

Tim thought he was a bad putter for several reasons. He was a good wedge player, good enough that he expected to get up and down whenever he missed a green. If he left himself a six-foot putt for par and missed it, he blamed his putting rather than the iron shot that missed the green in the first place.

Second, Tim hit a lot of greens because he was, indeed, very good with his woods and irons. That gave him a lot of birdie putts in the range of seven to fifteen feet. No one makes all of those. But Tim dwelt morosely on the ones he missed.

It's a natural trick of perception. If you're hitting the ball badly, you generally come into the clubhouse thinking that your putting wasn't so bad, and perhaps even saved you from a miserable round. If you're hitting the ball well, you're likely to focus on your putting as the only thing standing between you and a string of 62s. Tim frequently came off the course with a 69 or 68, feeling unhappy because he thought it should have been 64 or 65.

That, in turn, caused him to put more pressure on himself when he was putting.

I tried to get Tim to see his yips problem not as something that had happened to him, like a virus entering his system. It was a function of his own mind. It didn't own *him*. He controlled *it*.

I told him he had to be patient. He hit the ball well enough that he didn't have to make as many putts as some of the other players did. All he had to do was make one or two good putts per round to be in contention at most tournaments.

He needed, I thought, to master the trick of working less at his putting. His grinding—the long hours of practice, the effort to master a perfect stroke—was hurting his attitude rather than helping it. He was trying too hard to control everything that happened on the green. He had to understand the paradox that in golf, to gain some control over what happens, a player has to abandon the notion that he can control everything.

One day on the practice green at the New England Classic, Tim was telling me how badly he was putting. He was unhappy with what I'd been telling him. And all the while, he was stroking twelve-footers into the cup.

I put a foot in front of his putter, stopped him, and pointed out how well he'd been rolling the ball when he wasn't thinking about it, when he was thinking about what he wanted to get off his chest with me.

I told him that the next day, he ought to try to get into the same thoughtless frame of mind on the greens. I wanted him to simplify his routine—to read the green, then step up, take a look at the target, and stroke it. If it missed, wherever it went, tap it in and go on. All he could do on any putt was calm his mind, focus on his target, go through his routine, and roll it. Then he could accept what happened. That had to be all he tried to do.

If he wanted to think about putting, I said, he should start thinking of thinking himself as a good putter. He should start thinking only about making putts. His persistent complaining about his putting had become part of his problem.

Tim tried it. It wasn't an instant cure. In my experience there are no instant cures. But it was a turning point. He putted better for the rest of that tournament.

As he explored this new approach to putting, Tim found it feeling more and more natural. He talked to some of the best putters on the tour and found that only a few of them spent as much time practicing putting as he had been doing. That helped him to ease off the putting practice. Some days, he went to the course, warmed up, and then hit no more than a handful of practice putts to get the speed of the greens. Then he would go play.

He played with the attitude that the best thing that could happen on a given putt was he'd make it. The worst was he'd miss it. The best wasn't so great; the worst wasn't so bad. He stopped trying to force putts to fall and started trying to let them fall.

In short, his attitude toward putting became more like his attitude toward the long game. With the long clubs, he'd always been a player who saw a target, hit the ball, found it and hit it again. Mishits didn't bother him, because of his firm faith in his ability to hit the next shot. As he started to think that way on the greens, his putting improved. So did his scores.

In 1989, he was sixth on the money list. In 1990, he was eighth. In those years, he was not near the top of the PGA putting statistics, finishing about sixtieth each time. But he made a lot of putts.

Any golfer who considers himself a chronically bad putter can learn from Tim's experience. No doubt it's true that some players have a greater natural gift for putting than others. But, after all, how much of putting is physical? How hard is it to roll a ball along the ground?

Putting, perhaps more than any other stroke, is affected by attitude, by how the player thinks about putting, by his confidence. And no one is afflicted by nature with a bad attitude. That's something golfers choose to develop entirely on their own. Conversely, they could choose to develop a positive attitude about it. When Tim did, he won a lot of money and several tournaments.

I remember how excited he was when he won at New Orleans in 1989 and qualified for the Masters. I remember how proud he was when he won back-to-back at the Disney tournament in 1989 and 1990, giving him matching trophies for his kids, Christopher and Katie.

He had become one of the top players in the world.

But the road to the top isn't straight. Nor are there any guarantees about staying there. In April 1991, Tim missed the cut at the Masters and accepted an invitation from some friends to go turkey hunting in the Georgia woods. He spent a night in a hunters' cabin and during the middle of that night, he woke up covered with ticks. Most likely, some hunter the previous week had gone to bed with his hunting clothes still on and infested the bedding.

Within three days, Tim felt as if he had the flu. Worse, his hands were shaking. He was listless. He had no energy.

He went to his physician and had a blood test. It was negative. The symptoms persisted, although they varied in intensity. Sometimes he was wracked with arthritic pain. Sometimes he seemed almost well again.

He rarely had enough energy to practice. He kept playing the tour, but he was no longer the golfer he had been in 1989 and 1990. He wound up missing the 1991 Ryder Cup team by a sliver.

Tim went to more doctors. In 1992, he was diagnosed with Lyme disease; it caused arthritis to hopscotch unpredictably around his body. He went on courses of antibiotics and cortisone injections. Last year, a doctor told him he had Epstein-Barr virus.

Whatever the diagnosis, his golf continued to suffer. After the 1994 season, he lost his tour card. In 1995, he played the Nike

Tour. He hoped it would be a year of rehabilitation, after which he would rejoin the PGA Tour. But he missed the top ten on the Nike money list and he didn't get one of the spots available at the tour qualifying school.

There was nothing I could do about Tim's physical problems. I was concerned, though, with their effect on his attitude.

Sometimes, working with college athletes, I've seen cases where a kid breaks an ankle, can't play—and his grades plummet.

Logically, one would expect the opposite. Free of the obligation to practice for several hours every day, a kid ought to have more time to study, and his grades should go up.

But it turns out that athletes' minds don't work that way. Once an athlete is injured, his mind and mental energy tend to focus on healing, sometimes at the expense of everything else.

It seemed to me that Tim's illness affected him that way. During the years he played great golf, Tim's commitment to becoming the best was constant and consuming. Whenever I suggested something I thought would help, Tim was ready to do it, as long as it made sense to him.

After his illness came on, that wasn't always the case. I thought that in his situation, he ought to be careful to not risk exacerbating his health problems. I thought he ought to give up chewing tobacco, give up drinking caffeine, and get himself in the best possible physical condition. He's older now and he has to change some bad habits he could get away with when he was in his twenties.

He told me that he felt the tremors in his hands much less when he experimented with a long putter, the kind where the butt presses against the golfer's rib cage. I suggested he use it in competition. But Tim didn't want to do that. He would say that no one makes a lot of putts with the long putter. I'd reply that I'd seen Bruce Lietzke and Brett Ogle win with the long putter. And, besides, the ball doesn't know anything about the length of the shaft of the club that hits it.

For a long time, Tim and I butted heads about how he should respond to his illness. When I suggested changes in his lifestyle, he took it as an effort on my part to deny the reality of his symptoms.

I never doubted the reality of his illness. But I believe that people must do as much as they can to take personal responsibility for their health and success. I couldn't guarantee him that changes in his diet and habits would make him feel better and play better. But I felt they were well worth trying. He could find out if they'd help only by trying them.

Tim had reached the top by applying his will to the problem of his putting. The power of will has been the engine of every great athlete I've ever coached, of all the great people I've met. Success, I believe, is self-determined, even though there are times in life when it's easy to think that it's not.

Tim's illness brought on such a time. He would try to practice and hone his skills, but his body would get tired. He would start telling himself that the effort wasn't worth it. But it is at such times that a person finds out how badly he wants something.

Sometimes players who have been on top and had the ground crumble beneath them don't think they should have to start all over again. They don't want to face again the intense effort, hard work, and sacrifice they once were prepared to sustain.

Every individual goes through periods when he does a lot of the right things—practicing efficiently, thinking well—and gets no immediate, tangible results. This is the point where successful people bring to bear the powers of faith, patience, persistence, and will. Faith is the ability to believe without any tangible evidence.

• • •

I WISH I could end this chapter with the story of a great tournament Tim played to climb back onto the tour. I can't. He hasn't done it yet.

But I've seen signs recently that his old commitment is coming back. He's decided to play with the long putter. He's getting into better physical condition. He failed to make it through the PGA Qualifying School last fall, but he told me it wasn't because he putted poorly. His swing was just a little off that week.

I thought that was a good sign. Tim wasn't blaming his putting for his problems. And he knows that his swing will come back. His thinking is starting to remind me of 1989.

When Tim and I talk now, it's about how he has no other choice but to decide that he loves the challenge of overcoming his illness. I tell him that I have seen lots of players struck by injury or illness. Two results are possible. It can make him stronger, or it can make him weaker. He has to believe that in the long run, his illness will make him a better player, because it will make him twice as tough, mentally and emotionally.

More than ever, because of his illness, Tim needs to get back to the things he did well before he got sick. He has to spend some time each evening visualizing the great round he will play the next day. He has to get back to believing in himself.

He has to believe that there's nothing he can do about his illness other than the treatments his doctors prescribe. But he can still control his thinking. He can decide that this illness is going to tell him a lot about himself and his character. He can decide that whatever else happens, he is going to be proud of himself when it's all over.

If he can do that, then his illness cannot really defeat him. Nor will illness or injury defeat any golfer who can honestly tell himself that he did everything in his power to overcome it.

No. 9

How Byron Nelson
Won Eleven Straight

EVERY NOW AND THEN A SPORTS WRITER WILL MENTION MY ROLE IN helping a player prepare his mind to win a tournament. Quite often, the writer will imply that there is something new or mysterious about what I teach. I sympathize with the journalist's search for novelty, but nothing could be farther from the truth. I teach principles that great golfers have always known and practiced.

I know this because whenever I talk to the great golfers of the past, that's what their stories tell me.

Of all the records in the long history of the game, the two most impressive are Bobby Jones's Grand Slam of 1930 and Byron Nelson's streak of eleven straight victories in 1945. Unfortunately, Jones is no longer around to talk about what went through his mind in 1930. But Byron can talk about the 1945 streak, and if he is asked, he will.

I had a chance to visit with him not long ago at Fairway Ranch, his home in Texas. Of all the great players of his era, Byron is the one who strikes me as the happiest, perhaps because he knows the joy of sharing and giving. He shares himself and what he has learned, and he is always conscious of an obligation to give something back to the game. The day we spoke, he had just finished hosting an annual fund-raising pro-am for a golf scholarship in his name at Abilene Christian University. He wants to get the scholarship's endowment up to a million dollars, so it will be self-sustaining. He also is a very visible and active host at the Byron Nelson Classic each spring in Dallas. And he makes it a point to attend the Masters and the Ryder Cup and the other major tournaments each year, although he's now eighty-three. He knows that his presence at a tournament symbolizes the game's continuity and best traditions, although he's far too unpretentious ever to put it that way himself.

I knew that Nelson's streak must have demanded an enormously effective golfing mind. And I knew that perhaps the most arduous tournament of the eleven he won that summer was the PGA Championship at Moraine Country Club in Dayton, Ohio.

In those days, the PGA was a match play event, but it began with a thirty-six-hole qualifying tournament. Byron tied for the qualifying medal with Johnny Revolta at 138. He didn't have to qualify, but he played because there was a cash prize that went along with the medal. Byron's share of that pot came to $125, which he calculated would pay for a few more acres of the spread that eventually became Fairway Ranch. Then there were five rounds of match play, each at thirty-six holes. Byron beat Gene Sarazen, Mike Turnesa, Denny Shute, and Claude Harmon to make the finals, where he faced Sam Byrd, the former New York Yankee outfielder who switched sports and became an excellent professional golfer. By the end of the tournament Byron had played 204 holes, the equivalent of nearly three regular tournaments. He was 37 under par.

All of this occurred in sweltering August heat, compounded

for Byron by an aching back. Every night, he received heat, massage, and osteopathic treatment. "It was the toughest tournament I ever won," he said.

The key hole of the final match, Byron recalled, was the ninth.

Moraine's ninth hole is a 416-yard par four. In both the morning and afternoon rounds, Byron went for a pin that was cut in the back right portion of the green. Both times, he missed long and faced a difficult downhill chip from the rough. Both times, Byrd put his approach shot within ten feet of the hole. Both times, Byron could not stop his ball on the downslope and he wound up lying outside Byrd in three while Byrd lay two.

Both times, Byron curled in his putt. Both times Byrd, unnerved, missed his.

"I made those putts because I could see the line they were going to follow," Byron said.

That got my attention. Did Byron Nelson visualize his shots back in 1945?

"I could visualize the flight of my ball just like you could draw a string," he replied.

I asked him to elaborate.

Well, Byron said, he might walk up the fairway, facing an iron shot to a pin cut in the back right portion of a green and protected by a bunker.

Even though his normal ball flight was a draw, he didn't try to draw the ball over the bunker and into the pin. "I had learned in my practice how to fade it," he said, "I just thought about that, and—funny thing—my body did it.

"In my early years," Byron explained, "I thought a lot about mechanics. I was trying to learn a new way of swinging, because steel shafts had just been introduced. I thought that swinging those clubs required you to take the club straight back and turn and use the feet and legs and get away from pronation and taking the club too much inside, which you did with the old hickory shafts.

"My first job as a pro was in Texarkana, Texas, back in 1933. People wouldn't start to play till after lunch. So I had the whole morning to practice. There was nothing much else to do.

"I didn't have anyone to shag balls, and I couldn't have paid them if I did, because I wasn't making that much money. So I'd hit some 3-irons or 8-irons or whatever and then I'd take the club down and hit them back. I thought very hard about mechanics in those days.

"But I found that as my game got better, starting in around 1936, I'd practiced and worked enough so that it was like you were going to sit down at the table and eat a piece of steak. You take your piece of steak and your knife and fork and you don't think about how you cut your steak or how you feed yourself, any more than you would about how you put on your shoes and tie them. That's automatic. And I felt that was the way my game was. Automatic.

"I think that's the reason I played as well as I did—because I trusted my swing," he concluded.

I asked him if he had what today would be called a pre-shot mental routine.

"I always felt that I didn't have a very creative imagination," Byron said. "But now I look back on the way I played, and I did have a creative imagination. Golf was so different then. On one golf course there might be two or three greens that were real hard, two that were real soft and so on. You played a practice round to learn these things. Then, during the competitive round, you'd walk up to the ball and visualize, concentrate, whatever word you want to use.

"I looked for a faraway target—a tree, a house, a barn, a flagpole, maybe a bunker in the distance that I couldn't reach. And I'd look at that and I'd take the club away from that. And then, when I came back through, I'd try to make sure that the back of my left hand was going right to that target."

Was that his only swing thought?

"Yeah," he replied. "Basically it was. On short shots, I taught myself to think as if it was like pitching coins to a line the way boys do. I'd look at the target, and I never thought to myself, *Take a three-quarters back swing.* I looked at the target and relied on feel."

Between the time he felt he had mastered the swing and the time he reached his peak as a player, there were two more things Byron had to learn about the mental game.

One had to do with acceptance.

"If all good players would tell you the truth about it, when they were young and learning how to play, they got mad when they missed shots," he said. "I mean *mad.* Bob Jones had a terrible reputation as a kid—throwing clubs, and awful stuff. I never was bad about throwing clubs, though I won't say I never did it. But I would get upset—kind of boom-boom, though not ugly at anybody."

I asked how he had learned to get rid of his anger.

"When I was the pro at Texarkana, there was an older man there named J. J. Wadley, who had learned to play golf from Jim Barnes, the 1916 PGA Champion. He was a wealthy man and he liked me because I was a good, staunch Baptist and I didn't smoke and didn't cuss. And he was a good player for his age and he would, just by his example, kind of shame me once in a while.

"And then when I went to work as an assistant for George Jacobus at Ridgewood Country Club in New Jersey, I still had a little problem, and he would tell me, 'Byron, whenever you play, you need to not get upset and get mad. Don't ever let it carry forward to another shot.' "

And he took the counsel of his parents.

"My father and mother were a big help. They didn't play golf. They knew nothing about golf. But they could tell I was upset when I came home from a bad round. I wasn't being ugly about it, but they could tell I was upset. So then they'd talk to me about it, and they said, 'You're going to have to learn to get over it.'

"I believed my parents. They were wonderful parents. They were smart parents. And, also, you know, I believed in the Bible, and it said, 'Let not the sun go down upon your wrath.' It doesn't say you can't get angry. But don't harbor it.

"So it was a process of gradually educating myself."

After he learned to control his temper, Byron said, he felt as if he were cruising on the golf course. He felt as if he were driving his car at 60 miles per hour on an open road. He was comfortable and in control, even when adrenaline was pumping.

He still missed shots. But he realized that everyone was going to miss some shots. The key was to accept that fact and forget about the misses.

"I still think that players who are consistent are players who forget what happened," he said. "The next shot is what counts, not what happened. I see players who are going along real good and they mishit a shot and they'll be standing in the fairway, swishing that club back and forth, trying to figure out what they did wrong. That's a mistake."

He had one more refinement to add to his mental game before the streak began. At the end of 1944, Byron was already well established as a player, but he wanted to get better. He took inventory after that season and found that his mistakes tended to fall into two categories—poor chips or "careless" shots. He might, for instance, miss a short putt because he failed to follow his routine every time. So he made up his mind to practice harder on his short game, and to make sure his mind was completely focused on every shot in 1945. The result was the streak.

During 1945, Byron told me, he was so focused on the process of hitting good shots that he never knew how he had scored until after his round. He felt as if he played in a trance.

"I would come in and I'd have to go hole by hole on my scorecard, carefully, to realize what I'd shot. I didn't ever know if I was five under, three over, or whatever it was. I never carried that in my conscious mind," he said. "I never knew where I stood in a tournament."

That peak concentration lasted, he said, through the first two tournaments of 1946. One of them, the Los Angeles Open, was a semi-major in those days, and one Byron had always wanted to win. When he won it, and then won again at San Francisco the next week, he realized he had fulfilled all of his goals. He had won every important tournament there was to win. And he had amassed enough prize money to buy the ranch he had always dreamed of. He kept playing through the end of 1946, mainly because he had an endorsement contract with Mac-Gregor. But the trancelike state of concentration that had carried him through the streak was gone. And then he retired from tournament golf.

It was clear that Byron had, through experience and some helpful teachers, picked up virtually all of the fundamentals of golf psychology that I teach today. He had learned to trust his swing and not to think about mechanics as he played. He had learned to visualize his shots. He had learned the importance of his short game; he had learned to rely on feel near the greens. He had learned to accept the results of any shot and let go of anger and frustration. He had learned to stay in the present and not to worry about outcomes.

Only one thing still puzzled me. Byron had published a couple of golf instruction books in his heyday. Both were full of photographs and text about swing mechanics. Both ignored the mental aspects of the game that had obviously helped him reach the top. Why?

"Aw," he said, and smiled, almost sheepishly. "People didn't talk about that sort of thing in those days."

How Bill Shean Prepared

for the Club Championship

at Pine Valley

....

....

....

NOT MANY PEOPLE THINK OF AN AIRLINER AS A PLACE TO PRACTICE GOLF. But that is where an old client of mine, Bill Shean, did his best work getting ready for the 1995 club championship at Pine Valley.

I first met Bill about eight years ago. By that time, he was already an accomplished amateur golfer.

Bill started in the game the old-fashioned way, as a thirteen-year-old caddie at Hinsdale Golf Club, in his hometown in Illinois. His first weekend on the job, he made eight dollars. The following day, Monday, was the caddies' day to play. Using some old clubs that belonged to his father, Bill played with them—and lost twelve dollars. He decided he had better learn something about the game, and fast.

So he went to a drugstore and bought a paperback copy of Ben Hogan's *Power Golf*. Bill was a good athlete, adept at any game he tried, and inside of a year, with his self-taught swing, he was scoring in the high 70s. He was short and wiry, and he was constantly seeking ways to compensate for his lack of length. To this day, he tees the ball extraordinarily high because he once read a magazine tip from Arnold Palmer that suggested this was a way to get an extra ten yards.

He played high school golf, but he was not one of those boys who are groomed for the pro tour through lots of early lessons, the USGA junior program, and a college powerhouse. He went to the University of Michigan with an Evans Scholarship, provided by an educational fund for former caddies. When he graduated, he went into the insurance business. He became a true amateur golfer, balancing his passion for the game against the demands of a business, a growing family, and a church which he served as treasurer. He rarely touched a club from October to April, but his game slowly, steadily improved. He was a contender in club championships, and won a number of them.

But he could never push his game to the next level, the national level. He tried, but never qualified for the U.S. Amateur. After a while he decided that part of his problem was psychological. With his caddie's swing, he never quite felt he belonged in national competition. "I would," Bill said, "beat myself before I started."

About eight years ago, Bill read something I had written in *Golf Digest* and called me up. I invited him to come to see me in Charlottesville. We talked, as I usually do with a new client, and he told me what he thought of himself and his game.

I took him to the practice tee at Farmington Country Club and handed him a 5-iron. I asked him to picture a big banana slice and then step up to the ball and hit it. He did. Then I asked him to picture a draw. He did, and he hit that. Then a tight, controlled fade. Then a straight ball. He hit them all.

"Your skills are fine," I told him. "You hit the ball as well as any amateur I work with. You just have to believe it."

Some people, when they hear that sort of thing from me, may

be a little suspicious that I'm patronizing them. I'm not. I'm honest with people. If I start with a player who has a dysfunctional swing and a yen to break 70, I tell him that he needs to take swing lessons. But, quite frequently, the player who comes to me is someone, like Bill, whose physical skills are more than adequate for his aspirations. When I tell him that, though, I am often met with skepticism. It's intriguing that people are quite willing to believe a swing teacher who tells them their mechanics are all wrong. They have a hard time believing someone who tells them their mechanics are all right, but their mental game is not.

Bill, however, was receptive. So we talked a lot about two things: pre-shot routine and game plan.

Like most good players, Bill had worked hard on the physical aspects of a pre-shot routine—grip, stance, posture, and alignment. They are all extremely important for consistent shot-making, and the professionals I work with regularly check them. But they do it at home in front of a mirror, or on the practice tee. On the course, they want to be able to set up their bodies without much thought. Bill had reached the stage where he could do that.

Less accomplished players, though, should not shy from making meticulous, conscious attention to grip, stance, posture, and alignment part of their routines. It will pay off.

But Bill had little or no sense of the mental side of the routine, and that is the side I care more about. Even more than grip, stance, posture, and alignment, a sound, consistent mental routine is the foundation of consistency. So we worked on it. Before every stroke, I asked him to stand behind the ball and observe the situation. Assimilate the information about lie, wind, yardage, and anything else pertinent. Choose a club, trusting his first instinct. Pick out a target. Picture the shot he wanted to hit.

Bill, as it happens, has the kind of mind that readily visualizes a shot. Some players do. They can visualize as readily as they can turn on a VCR. Some players, though, do not. This is not a disadvantage. They simply have to look at their target and believe that the ball is going there.

Once Bill had the picture firmly in his mind, and believed in it, I asked him to take his address without delay, take one more look at the target, and let the shot go without permitting thoughts about his mechanics to interfere with his concentration on where he wanted the ball to go—in short, to trust his swing.

Those are the fundamentals of a good mental routine. They are the process that a good player commits himself to think about and to follow on every shot.

Then we talked about game plans. Golfers should have a game plan for every competitive round they play. A game plan breaks down the course hole by hole. It designates the club to hit on every tee and the target to aim at. Frequently, it designates the section of the green a player wants to hit with his second shot—or his first on par threes. For good players, it establishes threshold distances on par fives. Within a certain number of yards, the player will try to reach the green in two. If his tee shot falls short of the threshold, the plan tells him where to lay up to give himself the best third shot into the green.

It often helps to formulate a plan if a player looks at a hole from green to tee rather than the other way around. This perspective suggests where the sucker pin placements are and where it's best to aim for the center of the green. It suggests what type and length of shot a player wants to hit into the green. And that, in turn, suggests the best length and placement of the tee shot.

On a typical 490-yard par five, for instance, the weekend player may decide that he wants to hit his third shot from a level spot in the fairway, 100 yards short of the green, which is his normal wedge distance. How to negotiate the first 390 yards? It may be that the course architect has placed hazards that influence the choice. But all other things being equal, is the best strategy to try to hit a driver 240 yards on the first shot and leave 150 for the second? Or would the smart approach be a 3-wood off the tee, for 200 yards, followed by a 4-wood for 190?

It depends on the player. The important thing is to think these things through ahead of time, during the planning process.

Game plans, obviously, take into account a player's strengths. Bill, for instance, feels that the driver is the straightest and most reliable club in his bag. So he plans to use it often. For other players, an intelligent game plan might require ignoring the driver and teeing off with a 3-wood or an iron on certain par fours and fives. Short, tight holes, in particular, may call for less club off the tee. Why drive the ball on a 310-yard par four that's lined with woods, water, or sand? A 3-wood or 3-iron may keep the ball on the fairway more often and still leave only a comfortable short iron to the green.

Sometimes, golfers confuse a conservative game plan with lack of trust in their swing. On the contrary, a conservative game plan is designed to enhance the golfer's confidence on every swing. First of all, it removes the decision-making process from the heat of the moment. Once he's out on the course, he has the feeling he's just carrying out a plan he already knows is designed to give him the lowest possible score. He knows that every shot in his plan is within his capabilities. That eliminates a lot of potential doubt.

A conservative strategy joined to a cocky swing produces low scores. Reckless boldness joined to a doubtful swing is a formula for disaster.

Obviously, a game plan has to have some flexibility. You can't select a club for certain par threes until you know where the wind is coming from, and how hard. You can't hit the ball as far if the weather turns cold and damp as you can when it's warm and dry. In effect, a golfer has to have a Plan B and a Plan C for different weather conditions. But there must be a plan.

Bill Shean listened attentively to what I told him and went home to Illinois. Later, he reported what happened. The first dozen or so rounds he played, he was highly disciplined. He followed his pre-shot routine religiously. He stuck to his game plan. And his scores were lower—below the course rating for each of the twelve rounds.

But he discovered something else. Normally, Bill is a gregarious, pleasant golf partner. If he has guests, he wants to make sure that they enjoy themselves. But when he immersed himself in his pre-shot routine and his game plan, he felt he couldn't do those things. He became quiet and detached. It felt, he said, like he was working. He decided that he wasn't quite ready for the commitment I was asking for. And he by and large stopped doing what we had talked about.

This happens sometimes, and I understand when it does. Personalities differ. Brad Faxon and Lee Trevino can be gregarious and still concentrate; in fact, being gregarious helps them. Bantering with the gallery between shots relaxes them. Ceasing the banter delineates sharply the moment when their pre-shot routines begin. But others, like Ben Hogan, have to stay quiet and deliberate throughout a round.

Situations also differ. I don't have the same mental approach for a Sunday afternoon round with my wife and daughter that I have for a tournament round. Football teams aren't as intense for an August exhibition game as they are for the Super Bowl.

I advise amateurs to designate a few weeks of every year as their competitive weeks. They might be the weeks of the club

championship or some other competition. For a few days prior
to those competitions, they need to find a way—either a prep
tournament or some serious practice rounds—to reestablish
the habit of immersing themselves in process and game plan.
The rest of the year, they can play casual golf. But serious amateurs have to understand that in top-flight competition, they'll
be going up against people who play no casual golf, who try to
play with competitive discipline every time they step on the
course. Such people will have an advantage.

Bill understood that. At that time, in his late forties, he wanted
most of his golf to be casual. That was fine with me.

At roughly the same time he first met with me, Bill was invited
by an Illinois friend named Jay Berwanger (yes, the same
Jay Berwanger who won the first Heisman Trophy back in 1936)
to play a few rounds of golf at Pine Valley Golf Club in Clemen-
ton, N.J.

Pine Valley is not so much a country club as it is a retreat for
golfers. The ambience is almost monastic, except that in this
cloister, the services are held outdoors, on the golf course.
There is no pool and there are no tennis courts. The clubhouse
is an unpretentious two-story building with plain green curtains,
a lot of bare wood furnishing, and a sign near the front door
that prohibits Mulligans off the tee at No. 10. It is not the sort of
club that is likely to hold a Fiesta Night at fifty-five dollars per
couple.

The course this simplicity serves is widely regarded as the
most demanding test of golf in the world. It was planned and
built, with some help from the British architect H. S. Colt, by a
businessman and avid amateur golfer named George A. Crump.
In 1912, Crump decided that the players in the Philadelphia area

needed a new club, with a course that might be open and play-able a couple of months longer than the rest of the courses around, a course that would challenge them and sharpen their skills for national competition. Crump found a large, empty tract of land in the pine barrens of southern New Jersey, served by rail from Philadelphia. The soil was sandy and it drained quickly, so it would have the playability he wanted. The land rolled, providing lots of elevation changes. And there were marshes and ponds for water hazards. It was a beautiful canvas on which to design a golf course.

And Crump had very exacting design ideas. He wanted holes of every kind: a couple of drive-and-pitch par fours; a couple of long, heroic par fours; doglegs left and doglegs right; holes that played in every direction relative to the prevailing wind; holes with plateau greens and holes with greens set in valleys; a little lob of a par three and a long, stern, uphill, everything-you've-got par three. He wanted some open tee shots, where all the hazards are visible. And he wanted some blind tee shots, where the golfer looks out at an acre of sand, juniper shrubs, and pine scrub, aims at a tree on the horizon, and trusts that there is a fairway somewhere out there beyond the forecaddie.

Most of all, Crump wanted the course to be uncompromising. Every tee shot at Pine Valley must first carry an expanse of sand or water one hundred to two hundred yards long. There is, in fact, so much sand on the course that the club doesn't bother with rakes; there would have to be too many of them. Players simply smooth over their sand divots and leave their footprints. The fairways are velvety and reasonably generous, and there is little rough. But missing the grass is like entering a Siberian prison; extrication is likely to be difficult, unpleasant, and costly. Many of Pine Valley's holes seem to be shaped like bottles with the flag at the lip; the closer you come to the greens, the tighter they get. As time has gone by, and trees have grown in around each hole, the course has become still tougher. Its slope rating, from the back tees, is 153. Every now and then, during the club's annual Crump Cup competition, some guest will come in with a handicap of one or two and fail to break 100.

Bill Shean liked Pine Valley immediately. It was challenging. It was, he thought, a club for players, not a chief executives' club. When he was invited to join, he accepted.

Most years he made time to fly in for the President's Cup, the annual August stroke play championship for members. But though he played well on occasion, he never won. The 1995 President's Cup did not seem likely to change that. Bill's business had kept him busier than usual. He hadn't had as much time as he wanted to sharpen his physical skills.

So he decided that he would have to make up for that with his mental game. On the plane from Chicago to Philadelphia, he took out an index card and a yellow legal pad. And he recommitted himself to a sound pre-shot mental routine and a game plan.

On the index card, he wrote down his mental routine:

"1. Have fun. Focus on every shot."

This was a general reminder.

"2. Observe."

By that, he meant checking the lie, the wind, the yardage, the pin sheet and anything else that was relevant.

"3. Target. Club. Kind of shot."

He would pick out a target, pick a club, and decide how to work the ball—high or low, fade, draw, or straight.

"4. See it."

He would envision the shot, see it going through the air and landing. From short iron distance, he would envision the ball going into the hole.

"5. Feel it."

He would envision swinging the club. Sometimes he might take a practice swing. Sometimes he wouldn't. But he would not make a shot until he felt that the right swing was inside him.

"6. Trust it. Commit to it. Let it go. Give up responsibility for what happens to it."

He would refrain from thoughts about swing mechanics and believe in his ability. He would be decisive. He would step up and hit the ball without delay. And he would never berate himself for a bad shot.

Bill's mental routine was a sound one. It included a lot of steps that made it easier for him to be decisive.

To reinforce his commitment to it, Bill decided to keep a different, private kind of score. He would, of course, write down the number of strokes he had taken. But after each hole, he would also write down the number of strokes he had taken after faithfully following his routine. He might, for example, make four on a par three. But if he had followed his routine on each shot, he would write "4–4" on the scorecard and grade himself at 100 percent. Or he might par the hole but lose his concentration on his first putt. Then he would write "2–3" and grade himself at only 67 percent for the hole. He vowed that the percentage score was the only one he would keep running track of and care about.

This is not a system that would be used by a lot of the touring professionals I work with. They work hard on adhering to their processes, and writing additional numbers down would only distract them. But there are some highly organized, structured people for whom this can work. Bill is one of them. It's a matter of individual preference.

Then, on the yellow legal pad, Bill wrote down a plan for every hole. He made some general decisions first. He would not, for instance, plan on drawing the ball off any tee. His natural shot is a fade, and he didn't feel confident, given his lack of practice time, that he could work the ball right-to-left. Whenever he got in trouble, he would choose a safe, conservative route back to the short grass, even if it meant playing backwards. There is, for example, a small, nasty pit bunker in front of the green on the par-three tenth that the members, when they're in mixed company, call the Devil's Aperture. A ball that finds the D.A. generally comes to rest on a downhill lie. The golfer has a constricted swing because of the walls of the bunker. He's got to clear a ten-foot lip. And there is no relief backwards, since there is nothing between the bunker and the tee besides sand and scrub. Bill decided that if he hit into the D.A., he would simply declare it unplayable, tee another ball, and hit his third shot. The worst hazard at Pine Valley, he knew, was panic. He planned to avoid it.

Here is his plan for each hole, and how he executed it during the first round:

No. 1, 427 yards, par four.

This is a dogleg right, but Bill's first notation was "drive to the center." Since he normally fades his tee shots, there's a temptation to try to shorten the hole by playing close to the corner. In the past, he found that this kind of aggressive tee shot sometimes led to trouble, a big opening number, and a feeling, for the rest of the round, that he was playing from behind. So he opted for a conservative tee shot and hit one into the middle of the fairway.

Steep banks, sand, and trees flank the green. He decided to play for the middle of the green no matter where the pin was cut. His 6-iron was a little thin, leaving him on the fringe, short and right. His pitch up was weak, but he holed a fifteen-footer to save his par.

No. 2, 367 yards, par four.

This tight, straightaway par four is one of the longer 367-yard holes in the world, because the green sits atop a ridge, high above the fairway, guarded by a necklace of bunkers. Bill planned to aim his drive at a tree branch behind the left side of the green and fade it into the middle. He did. He wanted to leave his second shot on the green below the pin placement he anticipated, and he did, smacking a 7-iron to twelve feet. He made the putt.

No. 3, 181 yards, par three.

As with all but one of Pine Valley's par threes, the green here is an island in a heaving sea of calamity. Bill expected the pin to be toward the back of the green during the tournament, and his main concern was to make sure he did not go long or left trying to stick his tee shot close. He wanted to play for the center of the green and have an uphill putt. He did, and got his par.

No. 4, 444 yards, par four.

This hole features a blind tee shot, over a sandy waste and the crest of a ridge, to a fairway that veers right and drops sharply downhill. The second shot can be anything from a fairway wood to a 7-iron, depending on whether the tee shot catches the downslope. Bill planned to hit an aggressive left-to-right tee shot, carrying 235 yards to catch the downslope. That's about as far as he can hit it. His drive found trees on the right. Following the plan, he eschewed a risky shot toward the green and chipped back into the fairway, leaving himself a long iron to a back left pin.

Bill's plan called for an aggressive shot to a pin in that position, but the 3-iron he played was too much club, and the ball ran over the green. He chipped back close and made the putt for a bogey. In his second scoring column, he gave himself 3 of 5, judging that he rushed himself on the tee shot and made a mental error by overclubbing on his approach to the green.

No. 5, 232 yards, par three.

This is a titanic par three, over a chasm and a pond, sharply uphill, to a green set in the side of a slope. Anything that misses right winds up either in a pine thicket or a series of tough little bunkers that look like shark's gills cut into the side of the slope. It's a hole where a lot of balls are picked up.

Bill planned to play a driver and aim at the staircase that leads up to the sixth tee from behind the left side of the green, minimizing the chance of missing the green to the right. If he hit it straight and missed left, he would still have a chip to the pin and a chance for a par.

He hit it eighteen feet right of the pin and two-putted.

No. 6, 388 yards, par four.

Bill prefers to play this dogleg from the back of the tee area, because that eliminates any temptation to cut the dogleg off by driving down the right side and fading the ball. He planned instead to start his drive down the left side and cut it a little, making it to the corner and leaving a medium iron, slightly uphill, to a narrow green that slopes severely from right to left.

He hit his drive roughly where he wanted to and played a knock-down 6-iron that caught the green's slope and rolled toward the hole. He made a ten-foot putt for his birdie. On the card, he gave himself 3 for 3.

No. 7, 578 yards, par five.

The fairway on this long hole is essentially two grass islands, lined by woods and divided by sandy wastelands; the second, called Hell's Half Acre, begins about 300 yards from the tee and stretches for another 120 yards or so. Bill had a Plan A and a Plan B, one for a windless day and one if the wind was in his face. Into the wind, he would try to hit a straight, hard drive so he'd be able to carry the sand with his second shot. With no wind, he'd play a cut drive, which he felt was a little more reliable. Then he planned to hit whatever club would leave him a full wedge into the green.

There was no wind, but his routine broke down on the tee shot. He recalled afterwards that he had failed to make a decisive hip and shoulder turn into the ball. He pulled it left, into some trees. Again, he played conservatively on the recovery, chipping sideways back into the fairway. A lot of players, in his situation, might then have pulled a fairway wood out of the bag and banged it as far as they could. But Bill stuck with his plan, and played a 3-iron that stopped 120 yards—a full wedge—from the green. He pitched it to thirty-six feet and two-putted for a bogey. He gave himself 5 of 6.

No. 8, 319 yards, par four.

This is a tricky short hole. The second shot is invariably from a downhill lie to an undulating, narrow green that can look as though it's set on a low pedestal with beveled edges, surrounded by sand and rough. Bill had once seen an excellent player, a man who had been runner-up in the British Amateur, take a 12 at this hole, chipping futilely from one side of the green to the other. His plan reminded him that no matter where the pin was, he would ignore it and aim for the center of the green. He did, even though he was only seventy-two yards away. He took his par, and walked to the ninth tee content.

No. 9, 427 yards, par four.

The view from the tee is a trompe l'oeil, because the fairway looks narrower than it actually is in the landing area. Bill's plan was to aim for the right-center of the fairway. The green slopes from left to right, and holding it from the left side of the fairway almost requires a long draw, which he didn't want to hit. From the right-center, he was able to hit a 6-iron and keep it under the hole. He made his birdie putt from eighteen feet.

He was one under par again, but he didn't know it. Walking to the tenth tee, he focused instead on his percentage score. It was good, he decided, but it could be better on the back nine.

No. 10, 146 yards, par three.

A small green, surrounded by trouble. Bill's plan anticipated a pin cut short and right—perilously close to the Devil's Aperture bunker. He resolved to ignore it and shoot for the middle of the green, which he did, dropping an 8-iron eighteen feet past the hole and two-putting.

No. 11, 392 yards, par four.

Though this hole bends gently right, Bill planned to hit his drive as straight as he could, because trees to the left of the tee discourage a fade. From the middle of the fairway, he wanted to plant an iron just short of the pin and leave himself an uphill putt. He did, and parred the hole.

No. 12, 344 yards, par four.

This dogleg left is considered the birdie hole at Pine Valley, a hole that George Crump thought of as a pitch-and-run. But when he got there, Bill found that it had gotten harder by getting shorter. A front tee was in use, and the hole was playing about three hundred yards. That meant that a good drive would be followed by a half-wedge. Some players would have laid up with an iron to give themselves a full wedge, but Bill has great confidence in his driver, and used it. His sand wedge to the green left him thirty-six feet away, and he two-putted. As he walked off, he reminded himself not to let the failure to make birdie distract him, because three of the best and most challenging holes on the course were coming up.

No. 13, 448 yards, par four.

A long dogleg left, by way of green islands surrounded by woods and bleak, sandy wasteland. Bill planned to play this hole aggressively, because he rarely hooks the ball. The player who tries to shorten the hole by driving the left side and hooks it can easily find himself in an unplayable lie. Bill hit his drive long and straight. The second shot here, like the first, is designed to punish severely anyone who plays down the left side and misses even slightly. The safe route, for a lot of players, is to lay up short and right of the green and try to chip close for a par. But Bill had only a 6-iron into the green, from a lie that left the ball slightly above his feet. He aimed for the middle and let the lie curve the ball gently left, toward the pin. He had only twelve feet for his birdie, but missed the putt. Nevertheless, he gave himself 4 of 4.

No. 14, 184 yards, par three.

The builders of Pine Valley placed this green on an island in the middle of a marsh and set the tee on a hill high above. They filled in the water behind the green to make it a peninsula, now surrounded by trees. But it is still a hole with no margin for error and a hole that can quickly ruin a medal round. Bill's plan was to minimize the chance that the swirling winds above the hole could blow a good shot into the water. He hit a knock-down 5-iron to the green and two-putted.

No. 15, 591 yards, par five.

Bill planned to play this hole defensively. It's a long one, with a tee shot over water to a fairway that rises steadily, cants left to right, and narrows considerably as it goes. Only a handful of players have ever reached it in two. Bill had no chance to do this, so he thought carefully about where he wanted his second shot to end up. The farther the second shot goes, the steeper and more difficult the lie for the third. Bill decided to lay up a little short and leave himself between a 4-iron and a 7-iron into the green, but from a relatively flat lie. He did. On his approach, he ignored a sucker pin at the back right corner of the green. His thirty-foot birdie putt found the cup. That, he thought, was a bonus. But just such bonuses often accrue to players who stick to a conservative strategy that allows them to swing confidently.

No. 16, 433 yards, par four.

This hole tests the confidence a player has in his driver. It bends right, but the sandy waste in front of the tee is aligned so that a player who wants to favor the right side off the tee has to carry more than 200 yards of trouble before hitting the fairway.

A player can aim farther left and have to carry only 170 yards, but that leaves a much longer, downhill second shot to a green guarded on the right by the edge of the pond that's in play on Nos. 14 and 15.

Back in the airplane, Bill had felt the hole was made for his hard fade off the tee; he expected to hit anything from a 4-iron to a 6-iron into the green. But he was excited after his birdie at No. 15, and he cracked a long drive that left him only a 9-iron into the green. His ball stopped ten feet away, and he made the putt for another birdie.

No. 17, 338 yards, par four.

For the first time, Bill deviated from his game plan. He had intended to hit his driver again and cut it to follow the bend in the fairway. But the tees were up and he thought that another exceptionally long drive might run through the fairway into the woods. So he used a 3-wood instead.

This is the only kind of deviation I like to see from a game plan, a deviation in a conservative direction. A golfer who changes to a more aggressive strategy has usually got some doubts in his mind when he gets ready to swing.

Bill hit his 3-wood dead center, but it settled in a divot. Again, he changed his plan slightly. He had intended to hit a short iron to the front of the green, keeping the ball below the hole. But to make certain he got out of the divot, he hit a 9-iron and landed fifteen feet past the pin. He two-putted.

No. 18, 428 yards, par four.

The last tee box, high over the fairway, offers a view that can be either intoxicating or intimidating, depending on how a round has gone. The fairway is framed by woods, sand, and shrubs. In the distance, the green is visible atop a mesa, beyond a road, a stream, and a wreath of bunkers. There's a temptation to just belt away off the tee, but Bill's plan reminded him to hit more thoughtfully than that. He wanted to start the ball toward a yellow hazard stake in the distance and cut it into the middle of the fairway, well short of some bunkers that guard the right side. Then he would have a medium iron over the course's last sandy waste, the road, the stream, and the greenside bunkers to a green that slopes sharply, left to right and front to back. He hit the fairway with his drive and left a 6-iron twenty-five feet under the pin.

As Bill reached the green, a distraction ambushed him. Someone near the first tee called out that another competitor had shot 69. Bill started adding up his score. He realized that if he made his putt, he would have 66. Thinking about that, instead of his putting routine, he left his birdie putt well short. He managed to pull himself back into the present and finish with a 67.

It was easily the lowest competitive round he had shot at Pine Valley. But it was not a perfect ball-striking round; he'd been in the woods twice. He'd made some excellent putts, but holed only one from more than twenty feet. It was simply a solid round in which a good plan had helped him stay with his routine, avoid panic, and let the strengths of his game carry him.

He would go on to follow up that round with a 69 and a 73 and win the tournament by seven strokes. In the process, he established new competitive course records for thirty-six and fifty-four holes.

The tournament would be, he would later reflect, one of the warmest memories of his life. It would be a weekend when all the effort he had put into golf—improving his swing and his mind—came together and bore fruit. It would be a weekend when he proved to himself that his balanced commitment to family, work, and sport was compatible with excellence. It would be a weekend that told him the best things in his life were still ahead of him.

But none of those things were on his mind as he stepped off the eighteenth green that morning. An assistant pro, Jason Lamp, asked him what he had shot.

"Eighty-three percent," Bill said.

He had, he calculated, stuck with his mental routine and his game plan on 56 of 67 shots. It took him a moment to realize that Lamp wanted to know how many strokes he'd taken.

No. 11

How Billy Mayfair

Rebuilt His Confidence

BILLY MAYFAIR, WHO WON MORE THAN $1.5 MILLION ON THE PGA Tour in 1995, keeps a notebook in which he jots down ideas that emerge in the conversations we have over the course of a season. Here is what he wrote after our first session of 1995, a few hours before the start of the Phoenix Open:

"Enjoy what you're doing. Have fun."

This may seem like belaboring the obvious. Golf is a game. It's supposed to be fun. Any little boy knows that.

In fact, Billy Mayfair knew it when he was a little boy. But two weeks into the 1995 season, he'd almost forgotten it.

The previous season had not been a good one for Billy. He fell from 30th on the money list in 1993 to 113th. After January, he did not have a top-ten finish. He missed a lot of cuts.

In his first two events of 1995, at Hawaii and Tucson, he shot an 80 and a 79 and missed the cut both times. By the time we got together in the study of his new home in Scottsdale, Billy was in serious distress.

"I feel like I'm holding on by a thread, Doc," he said to me as we sat down. "I'm afraid I'm going to embarrass myself out there today."

Once he had said that, Billy's doubts and fears spilled out in a torrent. He was afraid he would never play well again. Or if he did play well for a few rounds, and got in contention, he was afraid he would blow his lead. He had a new bride, a new home, and he was afraid he was going to play his way off the tour.

He was particularly anxious about playing in Phoenix, where he grew up. Once, when he'd been the hot young phenom out of Arizona State, he'd felt as if he owned Phoenix. Now he felt that it had become Phil Mickelson's town.

All of this was said, of course, in a room that belied his words, a room filled with trophies he had won playing golf. Billy was a good player. I knew that. The problem was, he didn't know it anymore.

We would not, I realized, be leaving for the golf course immediately. We had some work to do right there before Billy could play tournament golf. He had to find his way again.

For Billy, the way started in the backyard of his parents' home when he was a toddler. He remembers his father putting a sawed-off club in his hands and teaching him to chip plastic balls around the backyard.

As a very young boy, he tried a variety of sports. But swimming competition paid off only in ribbons. Golfers won trophies, and Billy liked trophies. He was hooked.

The way led next to a great old municipal course in Phoenix called Papago Park. Built in the desert on the western edge of the city under some striking red rock cliffs, Papago was a tough, straightforward course with a driving range, and, most important, a big, rolling, crowned practice green.

The practice green became Billy Mayfair's playground. Every day after school, his mother would pick him up and drive him to Papago Park. He'd stay there until dark. Then it was back home, dinner, homework, and into bed.

Mondays through Fridays, Billy chipped and putted. That's all he did. From the practice green at Papago, he could look down at the practice tee and see boys his age whaling away with drivers. Look toward the south, and he could see the first tee, and there might be boys starting actual rounds of golf. It didn't matter.

Mondays through Fridays, Billy Mayfair was there to chip and putt. It was partly because the Mayfairs didn't have a lot of money to spend on greens fees and range balls. But it was mostly because Billy knew that chipping and putting would make him a better golfer.

There was one other kid at Papago Park who did the same things Billy did. That was Heather Farr, who grew up to be a star on the LPGA Tour before her life was tragically cut short by breast cancer.

It was no coincidence that the two kids who spent all their time on the practice green were the ones who went on to professional success. Skill with the wedges and the putter is what separates money winners from touring pros.

On weekends, Billy had a different routine. On weekends, the course's pro, Arch Wadkins, would let Billy pick up balls along the range and hit them for free. That was where he learned his long game.

And from a very young age, Billy competed. The Mayfairs scraped together money for travel and tournaments every summer and school vacation. Once, when he was a teenager, Billy spent Christmas Eve and Christmas alone in a Miami hotel room, because there was only enough money to send one member of the family to Florida for the Orange Bowl tournament.

He didn't mind that much. Billy was a shy, quiet, towheaded

kid, never a social butterfly. He knew that tournament golf was what he wanted to do, and he was willing to do whatever it took to play.

He went to Arizona State, and there he started to win national championships. In 1986, he won the U.S. Public Links Championship and in 1987, the U.S. Amateur. He was the college player of the year. Then he turned pro.

Billy knew what his amateur credentials meant as a pro. The PGA Tour players who had graduated from Arizona State had apprised him of that. "Here's a quarter," one of them had told him. "Go call someone who cares what you did as an amateur."

But he did well in the qualifying school and hung on to his card after his rookie year, 1989.

When I first noticed him, Billy was much like the unobtrusive kid who used to hang around Papago Park, chipping and putting. He wasn't one of the outgoing players on the tour practice tee. He kept to himself, said very little, and practiced a lot. You didn't see him out at night.

One of the big lessons he learned in his first year was taught, inadvertently, by Tom Kite. Tom won at Bay Hill that year. Billy finished back in the pack. Billy drove to the next tournament venue, the TPC at Sawgrass, and went out to the course Monday morning.

There was Kite, on the practice tee, less than eighteen hours removed from his win at Bay Hill, working hard on his game.

That, Billy decided, was someone to emulate.

The next year, 1990, his hard work started to pay off. He won nearly $700,000, more money than any second-year player in PGA history. He was a fixture on the tour for the next few years, winning for the first time in Milwaukee in 1993.

But in 1994, it started to go sour. The problem was that Billy tried to perfect his golf swing.

There is no bigger canard in golf than the old saw that practice makes perfect. It doesn't. Golf is a game played by human beings, and no matter how much they practice, they will remain imperfect. They will make mistakes.

Athletes who become self-critical perfectionists are flirting with trouble.

When their skills, inevitably, fail to meet their expectations, they can get tense and frustrated. They can begin to doubt their abilities. The more they practice, the worse they perform.

That was what happened to Billy in 1994. Moreover, in his determination to perfect his golf swing, he started to neglect his short-game practice. He'd stay at the range and beat balls until he was exhausted. In the little time he had left, he might hit a few putts, but that was it. He got away from the regimen of chipping and pitching that had brought him success as a boy.

ALL OF THAT, of course, was not something that could be remedied in the few hours we had before Billy's Phoenix Open tee time. I appreciated the candor and courage Billy displayed in confiding his fears to me. A lot of players would have been too proud to do it. I knew that as long as he recognized his problems, he had a good chance to solve them.

But at that particular moment, he didn't need a long-term program. He needed something to latch on to, a thought that could get him through the day and the week. He needed a ray of hope.

That's when I suggested that he resolve to enjoy himself.

Golf, after all, was a game he had always loved. He'd loved it when he was a boy, spending all those hours on the practice green at Papago Park. He'd loved it enough to want desperately to make it his career.

He could rediscover the pleasures of the game—the texture

and smell of freshly clipped grass on a sunlit day, the click that the ball makes when it's struck solidly, the deliciously long seconds watching a well-struck drive soaring against the sky, or a good putt rolling toward the hole. He could enjoy the camaraderie of competition and the friends he'd made on the tour.

That, in fact, is what I'd recommend to any player who is suffering a crisis of confidence. The first step ought to be the rediscovery of the joys of the game.

A golfer who actively appreciates the essential pleasures of the game is insulated from the ups and downs of competition. If he scores badly, it's not so terrible. If he scores well, that's great. But he doesn't need to score well to enjoy himself.

Billy went out and enjoyed himself in the Phoenix Open. And, not coincidentally, he started to play better. He played so well, in fact, that he almost won. He tied with Vijay Singh and lost in a playoff.

When he called me that Sunday night, though, he didn't sound like a loser. He was thrilled. He'd won enough money to assure himself of keeping his card. More important, he'd proven to himself that he could still play.

I wish I could take credit for that, but the truth is that even a player who thinks his confidence is totally shattered, or his swing is totally fouled up, can in reality be just a half inch away from his old self. It can be a literal half inch, if we're talking about the swing plane. Or it might be a figurative half inch, if we're talking about confidence. Billy really didn't have as far to come back as he thought he did.

And I wish I could take credit for the next step that he took to restore his game, but again, I can't. Billy went out to San Diego two weeks after the Phoenix Open. He was paired the first two days with Peter Jacobsen, who'd just won the AT&T at Pebble Beach.

"You haven't done that well in five years," Billy asked Peter. "What happened?"

Nothing magical, Jacobsen replied. He had just dedicated himself to his short game over the winter months.

I, of course, had often mentioned the short game to Billy. He'd known about it since his youth. But there's nothing like hearing it from a player who's just won. Billy rededicated himself to his short-game practice regimen. Within a couple of months, he started to feel that his short game was back.

And the short game is usually great medicine for an ailing golfer. **The best remedies for a golfing slump, I've found, are putting things back in perspective, dwelling on the positive, looking for something good to happen—and rededication to the short game.**

THE IMPROVEMENT WAS immediate and noticeable. Billy found that on days when his long game was not perfect, good chipping and pitching helped him score decently. On days when his long game was on, it helped him go low. He finds that a lot of the par fives on the tour are just beyond his reach in two shots. That leaves him with a lot of twenty- or thirty-yard pitches. He started to get a lot more of them close enough to make birdies.

He rediscovered that a good short game helped take the pressure off his long game and his putter. He found that when he missed a green, he would calmly hand the club back to his caddie and walk toward the hole thinking that he might chip his third shot into the hole, and that he could at least make par.

He stopped thinking, *Oh gosh, here comes another bogey.*

He changed his practice philosophy. If his swing didn't feel exactly right, he stopped fighting it, figuring that it would be better to let it rest overnight than to keep on beating balls and ingraining his mistakes. He spent the extra time practicing his chips, putts, and pitches. He decided that true discipline, at times, meant that he stop hitting balls and get some rest rather than keep practicing until he was exhausted.

In July, he won the Western Open, his first victory in almost two years. He had several more top tens and a couple of near misses.

He had a good chance to win the World Series of Golf in September. After three rounds, he was in fourth place, three behind Vijay Singh and one behind Jose Maria Olazabal and Jim Gallagher, Jr.

He scorched the front nine with a 32, and he opened a three-stroke lead on the field by the time he reached the tee at No. 15.

And there, he suddenly started thinking that he was going to lose the golf tournament. He had a premonitory vision of himself sitting in front of his locker, head down, sad and disgusted.

He bogeyed the next three holes. He missed a six-foot par putt on No. 15. His sand wedge approach to No. 16 was perhaps too aggressive, and he bounced off the hard surface into the rough. He was over the green on No. 17. He was tied for the lead with Greg Norman and Nick Price, who were coming on strong.

Billy steadied himself and played No. 18 beautifully, hitting his approach to eight feet. His birdie putt, which would have won the tournament, was well struck. It veered right at the last instant and lipped out.

On the first playoff hole, Norman chipped in from sixty-six feet away for a birdie that neither Billy nor Nick could match. Ironically, it was someone else's short game that beat Billy.

"I had the golf tournament in my hand," Billy told the press afterwards. "And I lost it."

. . .

THE LOSS WAS still fresh in Billy's mind when he came to the Tour Championship at Southern Hills Country Club in Tulsa in the last week of October.

Conditions were tough in Oklahoma that week. It was cold. The wind, as Rodgers and Hammerstein would have put it, came sweeping down the plain. The greens were dry and hard to hold. It was not the same course that Nick Price had played in 11 under par in the 1994 PGA. Even par was going to be a very good score.

Billy was ready. He had spent the previous week thinking about Southern Hills and thinking about playing it in cold, windy weather. When he got to the course and saw the flags stiffly snapping in the gale, he thought to himself, *Yeah! This is what I prepared for.*

I talked to Billy by telephone just before the tournament started. We talked about the usual pretournament ideas: staying in the present, staying committed to routine, being patient. We talked about the thoughts he had to change if he wanted a better outcome than he'd had at the World Series. We talked about being ready to win.

Billy opened up with a 68 and stayed near or in the lead for the next two days. On Saturday, he shot a 69, and the second-round leader, Brad Bryant, struggled to a 73. Suddenly, Billy was the fifty-four-hole leader, and by the same three-stroke margin he had lost at the World Series.

We talked each night during the tournament, and I emphasized how a tough golf course like Southern Hills, especially in unfavorable conditions, demands patience. There were going to be bogeys. Players had to resist the urge to get too bold in an effort to make up for them.

Billy was nervous about his three-stroke lead. He had never

had that kind of margin after fifty-four holes. He felt it put more pressure on him and reduced the pressure on everyone else.

"Is there," I asked, "anyone in the field who wouldn't trade places with you? Anyone you'd trade places with?"

"No," Billy said.

"Well, then," I said, "let's be glad you have that three-stroke lead. And let's be totally prepared to win tomorrow."

It wasn't easy for him to do that. A lot of players who think perfectly well in run-of-the-mill tournaments have the misimpression that it takes something different to win a big event—a major championship, a World Series, a Tour Championship. It doesn't. The players who win big events are usually players who are comfortable enough to think exactly as they do in lesser events, to stay with their routines and stay in the present.

Billy had to literally talk himself into being that way. When he woke up Sunday morning, he told himself, "This is your golf tournament. You're going to win this golf tournament."

He stepped to the window and looked at the flags outside the hotel. The wind, he estimated, was already blowing at 30 miles per hour.

"No matter how the wind's blowing, you're going to win this golf tournament," he told himself.

When he stepped onto the first tee, and when he stepped up to virtually every shot that day, it was the same thing. "You're going to win," he told himself.

Normally, this kind of thought might not be helpful. It's oriented toward results, toward the future. But in Billy's case, I would make an exception. He wanted to avoid a repetition of the World Series. He didn't want to think about losing. Telling himself he would win was a way of preempting such thoughts. Then he took care to return to the present and get into his routine.

The first tee at Southern Hills, like the first tee at Riviera, sits high above the valley, where the bulk of the course is. The wind had blown Billy's drives into the rough in each of the first three rounds. But on Sunday, it had shifted behind him, and he needed only a 3-wood. He hit it down the middle, 110 yards from the green.

The ball came to rest in a divot. He hit a wedge, but he couldn't spin it, and it rolled to the back edge of the green. "One shot at a time. Stay in your routine," he told himself.

He chipped to about six feet, made the putt for par, and he was on his way.

At No. 2, with the wind howling from left to right, he drove the ball into trees on the right side of the hole. He felt surprisingly unruffled. He thought he had an opening to the green and he went for it. His ball hit a tree and bounded out into the fairway. Still unperturbed, he hit a sand wedge to ten feet and made that putt.

It's amazing how patient and composed you can be if you believe you're going to win. When a golfer is in the right state of mind, missed shots mean little to him.

Billy told me later that if he hadn't prepared his mind to win, he probably would have stepped up to those first two putts worried about making bogey, worried about letting his lead slip away. Instead, he addressed them thinking only of making them, of finding a way to score well.

He kept making pars as the rest of the field slipped back. At No. 15, he hit a good drive, but it kicked off a mound and into a tough fairway bunker. He had two choices. He could hit a sand wedge and make sure he got out into the fairway. Or he could try to reach the green with a 4-iron. The latter was a risky shot. If he got the ball to the green, but left it a little right, he could face an impossible chip downhill and be looking at the possibility of a double-bogey.

For the first time that day, he decided he needed to know where he stood. He asked his caddie.

"You're five strokes up," the caddie replied.

Billy put the 4-iron back in the bag and hit the sand wedge. He made bogey, and another bogey at seventeen.

Still, he had a comfortable lead on the eighteenth tee. He picked out a tower on the horizon, aimed at it, and went through his routine. Then he let the shot go. It was down the middle. He had 185 yards left, over a bunker, and he picked out a pillar in the clubhouse as a target. He swung and watched the ball clear the bunker. The celebratory roar from the crowd told him all he needed to know. The ball was on and close.

He had, indeed, won the golf tournament.

AFTERWARDS, BILLY PHONED and told me about something he'd seen on television in Phoenix. Charles Barkley of the Phoenix Suns, a good friend of Billy's, had been on. The interviewer asked Barkley what he thought about his friend Billy Mayfair's "dream season."

"I wouldn't call it a dream season," Barkley said. "That makes it sound like he won't have another one."

That answer pleased Billy. In fact, in the season of his dreams, he wins all four majors. So he won't be content with what he achieved in 1995. He has a lot left that he wants to accomplish.

He's certainly in a stronger position to try to achieve those dreams than he was at the beginning of 1995. He has been through the fire.

All great athletes, I think, have had to go through a period of fire, a period of despondency and near despair. The fire is like the smelting process that burns ore and turns it into precious metal. Without the fire, the process cannot happen.

An athlete who has gone through what Billy did and come out the other side is stronger. He knows that come what may, he is tough enough to bounce back.

And that, like a good short game, is an enormous asset.

No. 12

....

How Dicky Pride

Crossed the Fine Line

....
....
....

GOLF IS A GAME OF SMALL GRADATIONS. THE DIFFERENCE BETWEEN A good drive and a drive out of bounds can be a few millimeters of change in the swing plane. The difference between making a living on the tour and looking for another line of work can be as small as a stroke a round.

So it is with the mental game. Players who win may think only slightly differently from those who don't. They trust their swings absolutely; others occasionally entertain a few little doubts. They marshal the right thoughts and attitudes on nearly every shot; others admit distractions several times a round. Those subtle differences can have an enormous impact on results. A good mind can be the difference between struggling in golf's minor leagues and winning on the PGA Tour.

In fact, it frequently is the difference. If you were to go to Florida sometime and happen upon one of the golf courses where the Tommy Armour mini-tour events are held, you might be hard-pressed to tell what level of golf you were watching. The players on the Tommy Armour Tour nearly all have impressive games and swings. They hit the ball a long way. They have all the shots. They sink a lot of putts. The only quick way to distinguish them from PGA Tour players would be the accoutrements of their game: They ride in carts, because they can't afford caddies, and they probably haven't sold advertising space on their shirt sleeves.

The difference between them and PGA Tour players is largely mental. Tour players have learned to think in ways that enable them to win. Mini-tour players by and large haven't. Good thinking can make a difference of a stroke or two a round, and that is all that separates minor leaguers from major leaguers in golf. It's a fine line.

Dicky Pride can testify to that.

I first saw Dicky years ago at the North River Yacht Club course in Alabama, where *Golf Digest* held some schools. He was always out on the practice range, hitting balls. He wasn't the sort of young golfer who would impress casual watchers as someone with great potential. Most people are impressed by great length on the practice tee, and Dicky didn't have that. He's of average size, and his good drives generally went 250 or 260 yards, with a little fade. He looked like the kind of kid who would have to scramble to make a good college golf team.

In fact, that's what he was. Dicky grew up in Tuscaloosa, where his father was in the real estate business. Dick Pride was a good amateur golfer and for a few years the coach at the University of Alabama. He taught Dicky the fundamentals.

Dicky was a fine basketball player in high school and a good golfer, but not good enough to get scholarship offers from any major colleges. He enrolled at Alabama, in his hometown. For a year or so, he never touched a club.

In the summer between his first and second years in college, Dicky got the bug again and started playing. He tried out for the golf team that autumn as a walk-on. He made it. He averaged 78 that season and never made the traveling squad.

But he kept plugging away. He spent a summer working at the Elk River Club in the North Carolina mountains, where he met his swing teacher, Todd Anderson. He read books by Tom Kite and Bob Toski. He took one of the critical steps a golfer who wants to get good has to take: He realized he had to improve his short game, and he started spending more time on chipping and putting than he did on his full swing.

He tried out for the golf team again and made it. But the first time the coach held qualifying for the traveling squad, Dicky shot 87. He was still terribly inconsistent, but he kept at it. The next semester he averaged about 75 in competition. He got his scholarship.

Dicky never thought of playing professional golf until his last year at Alabama. He started to display a talent for playing well on tough courses. He qualified for the U.S. Amateur in 1991. He got to the semifinals—a remarkable performance for someone who had been a questionable choice to make the Alabama golf team a year earlier. He might have gotten to the finals, except that on the seventeenth hole, he let his thinking escape from the present.

He was one up. He hit his drive into the fairway and his opponent drove into the rough. Like a temptation from the devil, a distracting thought entered his mind: *Wow! Win this hole and you go to the Masters.* (The finalists at the U.S. Amateur automatically get invitations.) Just as Davis Love III stopped playing well when he started thinking about the Masters, Dicky started making mental mistakes. He pushed his 7-iron lay-up shot to the right and into a bunker. His next shot flew the green. He made a double-bogey and lost the match in a playoff.

Dicky went back to school and played well in his senior year, though not well enough to be an All-American. No one thought of him in the same class as Phil Mickelson or David Duval, who were the top collegians at the time. Except Dicky. He had started to believe he could do something in golf.

In 1992, he qualified for the U.S. Open. He went to Pebble Beach and shot 83 and 88. But that experience was enough to persuade him that he could compete on the highest level. Dicky had a good mind.

He turned pro later that year, went to Florida, and joined the Tommy Armour Tour. After he won his first event down there, he came north to Charlottesville to see me.

Not many people would have bet much money on Dicky's chances of making it to the PGA Tour at that stage. But I didn't care what his credentials were. First of all, it's not my job to care. It's my job to help people realize their potential, and to do that, I have to treat each of them as if they have unlimited potential. As I told Dicky:

It's not very important where you've been. Life is about where you're going.

And I could see that Dicky had some talent. The ground was covered with snow, and it happened that Brad Faxon was visiting. I took them down to the University, to the gym where I have my office. We did some putting on an indoor course. Brad had to drain two long putts on the last two holes to beat Dicky. And Brad was one of the top putters on the tour.

More important, I could tell from the stories Dicky told me that he had a good attitude about himself. Given his scant accomplishments as an amateur, he had to have a good attitude just to think he had a chance to make it on the tour.

Dicky already understood some of the fundamentals of the mental game. He already had a sound routine. He didn't burden himself with thoughts about swing mechanics while he was on the course. He thought about where he wanted the ball to go.

We talked about a long-range philosophy that could carry him from the mini-tours to the big tour. Dicky is an intense, wired young man. He needed to understand that golf is a game that rewards steady, continuous effort far more than short bursts of passion. I suggested a goal for him: to improve a little every day. If he could do that, the rest would take care of itself.

I told him that success wasn't a matter of how much he knew about the mental game. Lots of people know the principles. It's a question of who applies those principles consistently and who applies them at the right moment. Psychiatrists and physicians, for instance, get great educations about the ailments, mental and physical, that afflict human beings. They understand how to stay healthy. Yet their suicide rates are among the highest in the country. Knowledge isn't much good unless you use it.

Of course, we talked a lot about the challenge he would face that fall in the tour's qualifying school. Every year, nearly a thousand very good young golfers pay their entry fees and embark on the q-school process. After a round of regional qualifying tournaments, the best of them spend six tough days in the final stage. At the end, the top forty and ties get cards that entitle them to play the tour.

I told him it would actually be a little easier to do well in the qualifying school than it was on the Tommy Armour Tour. That's because a lot of players think they can do well on the Tommy Armour Tour. Not so many really believe they can do well at the qualifying school.

That fall, Dicky had his mind in the right place during the first stage of the school. He called me up one night and recounted how he'd almost gotten into a fistfight with someone who wanted to talk to him after the third round about what he would have to shoot to make the finals.

"You're in great shape. All you need to shoot tomorrow is—" the man said.

"I don't want to know," Dicky said. He was determined not to start playing with one eye on the scoreboard.

"But, Dicky, all you have to do is—"

"I don't want to know," Dicky interrupted him again.

After a few more, increasingly louder, exchanges, the man finally got the message. Dicky didn't want to know.

He played excellent golf in the final stage, opening with a 70 and following that with 71, a 64, a 72, and a 68. He faltered a bit in the final round, three-putting several holes in a row. But Tim Simpson, who was playing with him, told me he was impressed by how well Dicky buckled down, stuck with his routine, and kept his composure. He birdied the sixteenth hole and came in with a 77, for an overall total of nine under par. He got his card. He was no one's All-American, but he had made it to the tour ahead of a lot of players who were All-Americans.

LIFE ON THE tour was a challenge of a different order. It was not so much a question of nerves as of intimidation. In Dicky's first tournament, in Hawaii, he felt as if he had held his breath through the first nine holes, waiting, perhaps, to wake up. He missed the cut in his first six events.

He made a cut and a three thousand dollar check at Bay Hill, then missed a couple more cuts. He took a few days off to go to the beach with his fiancée, Kim Shearer. He told her how depressed he was. He told her how hard he'd been practicing and how little it seemed to help. He told her he didn't think he had the talent to play on the tour. He was nearly in tears.

Kim did a wise thing. She told him to stop whining and start acting like the guy she'd met when he was playing the Tommy Armour Tour. Back then, Dicky had been cocky. He needed to get cocky again, she said, and start playing the way he was capable of playing. Dicky went to Houston and made another cut and another check. His confidence was slowly coming back.

I saw Dicky shortly after that at Byron Nelson's tournament. We talked for a while about his putting. I told him he had to stop thinking so much about whether the ball was going into the hole and stop caring whether he struck the ball perfectly and gave it the classic overspin roll as he sent it on its way. He needed to concentrate on getting the line and the speed and letting the results take care of themselves.

Dicky finished in the top twenty at the Byron Nelson, which was shortened by rain. He was slowly getting more comfortable, but he was still on a roller coaster. He was up one week and down the next. The New England Classic was a down week. He missed the cut again. His wrist was sore. He missed his plane out of Boston on Friday night and didn't get into Memphis until Saturday.

Dicky's exempt status was low enough that he wasn't certain he'd get into the field at Memphis. On Saturday, he didn't try to play a practice round. He just walked the course, making notes for his game plan. He carried a putter and a few balls, and he made certain to hole at least five short putts on every green. That day, he must have watched 150 of his putts roll into the cup.

He kept practicing, but he didn't learn for certain that he would be in the field until Lee Janzen dropped out on Tuesday. I think that helped him. It kept his thoughts focused on his desire to play, not on whether he could make the cut. His attitude was, "I'm hitting the ball well. I just need a chance to show it."

In fact, there was a concatenation of good influences on his mind: the putts he made on the first day he walked the course; the wait to see whether he could play; and even the playing

partner he drew for the first two rounds, Howard Twitty. Howard is tall and lanky, with a slow, ambling stride. Dicky let that
slow, steady walk set a calm, deliberate mood for him that lasted
nearly all week.

He opened with a 66, despite bogeying the last two holes. He
kept playing well, though not without some misadventures. He
snap-hooked the ball into the water on the eighteenth hole on
Saturday, but he was still tied for the fifty-four-hole lead.

Dicky was a self-described nervous wreck on Saturday night.
He called me from his hotel room.

"Doc, the eighteenth hole is driving me crazy," he said. "I've
hit it in the water there twice. I can't get myself to stop thinking
about it."

There was only one thing he could do, and that was to con-
front his fear of the eighteenth. I told him to visualize the tee
shot he wanted. He needed to see the club he would use, the
swing he would make, the flight of the ball, the spot where it
landed. He needed to hear, in his mind, the hush before he let
the shot go and the reaction of the crowd as the ball took off.
He needed to smell the grass and feel the sweat trickling down
his neck.

That helped a little bit. He went to bed, but he felt hot, so he
got up and turned the air conditioning on. Then he remembered he can't sleep with air conditioning on. He couldn't get
back to sleep. At breakfast time, he could barely eat. Then he
had an unanticipated delay before teeing off, and by the time he
addressed the ball for the first time, he felt as if he were inhaling
a strange gas—certainly not oxygen.

Dicky pushed a weak tee shot right of the bunkers on the
right side of the fairway. Then he hit a 5-iron that jumped long,
winding up on a downslope behind the green. He was looking
at a chip that he would normally have felt lucky to stop within

ten feet of the hole. As he addressed the ball, he didn't feel right. He considered, for a second, backing off. Then he caught his attention and forced it back to the business at hand, imagining the target and the ball going in. He swung fearlessly and flopped the ball onto the green. It trickled in.

There's no question that holing out like that on the first green can ignite a round. It's not just being lucky. Holing a shot like that can inject confidence into a nervous player's mind. It can help him to play his best golf the rest of the way.

Dicky was still struggling a bit, driving into the rough and laying up in the wrong spots. But he managed to hold his round together through the turn.

On No. 10, he hit a good drive into the fairway and had a 6-iron left. For the first time that day, his mind slipped out of the present. He thought about everything that would come to him if he won, beginning with the trip to the Masters. It was the same distraction that had beguiled him a few years earlier at the U.S. Amateur, and his mistake had similar consequences. He hit a poor shot over the green into a nearly impossible position.

Dicky lost his composure.

"I'm not going to let myself do it again!" he yelled at his caddie. "I did it to myself once and I thought myself out of the Masters, and I'm not going to do it again!"

His caddie, of course, had no idea what Dicky was yelling about.

He hit a lob wedge that only reached the fringe of the green. Then he made the putt. As with his chip-in on the first hole, the putt from the fringe helped him recover his focus. It did not waver the rest of the way.

He birdied eleven and lipped out putts on thirteen, fourteen, and fifteen. He told himself that the near misses only showed that he was putting well. He birdied No. 16 and tied for the lead again. On No. 17, he hit a 3-iron into the green, thinking that he would cut it and work it in toward the flag from the left side. The ball went dead straight. He caught a bad break in the rough. His ball was on an exposed root. He couldn't get his chip closer than thirty feet, and he made bogey.

That's all right, he told himself. He had made a bogey, but not a mental error. His pre-shot routine was still exactly what it should be.

So he came to the eighteenth tee needing a birdie. The tees were up, the fairways were hard, and the hole is a dogleg left. A long drive, from the forward tee position, could go through the dogleg. Dicky pulled out his 3-wood. He called to mind all the positive images he had conjured up the night before, went through his routine, and hit a perfect tee shot, into the center of the fairway, 167 yards from the hole.

He was excited, and he realized it. So he took a bit less club than he might otherwise have done, a 7-iron, and hit it twenty feet from the hole.

Jay Haas was Dicky's playing partner. He had fallen out of contention, but did something elegant on that last hole.

"Enjoy this," he said to Dicky as they stood on the green. "This is what you play for."

It was exactly what a rookie would want to hear from a veteran at that moment.

Dicky lined up his putt, went through his routine, and stroked it. For an instant he thought he had left it short. But it struggled up to the hole and fell in. For about ten seconds, he screamed his jubilation at the top of his lungs, letting out the accumulated tension of the final round. No one could hear him over the roar of the crowd.

He had shot 67 for a 17-under-par total of 267. He was in a playoff with Hal Sutton and Gene Sauers.

Dicky played the playoff hole, No. 18, exactly as he had a few minutes before—3-wood, 7-iron to twenty feet. Sutton and Sauers also reached the green in regulation. Sauers missed his putt, leaving it an inch or so short.

As he prepared to hit, Dicky felt awash in confidence. He knew his target should be the right lip. He knew if he got the ball to the hole on that line, it would go in. He thought, he later told me, about something I'd once said: that golfers under intense pressure tend to hit woods and irons long and leave putts and chips short. He thought about getting freer and cockier. He told himself, "nothing but net." And he stroked a firm, bold putt that hit the center of the hole, popped against the back of the cup, and fell in.

Sutton missed his birdie putt, and Dicky had gone from being a nonentity to a winner on tour.

He received a photograph in the mail shortly afterwards. It was a picture of the scoreboard at a 1992 amateur event called the Cardinal Invitational. It showed Dicky Pride in forty-fourth place with scores of 72, 79, and 73.

"What a difference a couple of years make," the tournament organizers wrote.

I thought they should have written, "What a difference the right state of mind makes."

But as quickly as Dicky got himself into the right state of mind, he got out of it. He recorded no more top-ten finishes in 1994, and he did not win in 1995. Were it not for the two-year exemption he got for winning at Memphis, he would have had to go back to qualifying school.

After winning, Dicky's expectations of himself were higher. He wanted so badly to do it again that he tried perhaps too hard.

When he hit a shot that didn't measure up, he tended to become self-critical and impatient. This happens quite often after a player wins a first tournament or a first major. Dicky had to learn to leave his new expectations behind when he stepped onto the course.

And there were changes in his life that affected his game. He bought his first home and his first car. His success led to invitations for outings and other distractions that he'd never had to deal with before.

We've talked recently about ways that Dicky can manage his schedule to enhance the chances that he will regain that optimal mental state he attained in Memphis. He's scheduled checkup visits with Todd Anderson every four to five weeks, primarily to make certain his setup and posture are correct. That way, he shouldn't find himself trying to compete when he's got doubts about his mechanics. We're going to see each other every month or so and talk periodically on the phone to make sure his mental game is where it should be.

He's scheduled periodic rest breaks. We've tried to make certain that his wife and his career are his top priorities. The time he has for socializing with his friends has to be subordinated to those priorities.

And we've talked about being consistent about practice time. He has to work out a schedule that gives him time around a practice green every day, or his short game won't be where it has to be.

If he doesn't feel ready to play great golf, he's going to stay at home until he does. He won't show up just because there's a tournament.

We want to make certain that when he competes, he's ready to trust equally in all parts of his game. Last year, it seemed that every week there'd be some part of his game he wouldn't trust

—his driver, his wedges, or some aspect of his putting. That has to end.

But even if he does all those things, he will not automatically recapture the mental edge he had in Memphis.

The hard fact is that the optimal state of mind isn't an object that a golfer can acquire, own, put on a shelf, and take down for use whenever it's required.

Rather, it's a condition that can be fragile, ephemeral, and maddeningly elusive. It emerges from the confluence of a lot of factors, some very subtle. And the factors vary from golfer to golfer. The best a golfer can do is ascertain as best he can the factors that work for him and strive to make certain they are present every time he competes.

The optimal state of mind is something a player must work on patiently, every day.

No. 13

······································

How David Frost Learned to Close

···
···
···

ONE OF THE HIGHEST COMPLIMENTS A PROFESSIONAL GOLFER CAN receive is to be known by his peers as a closer. A closer is someone who puts tournaments away, who wins when he gets into position to win.

My friend David Frost is a closer.

Frosty is by no means one of the longer hitters on the PGA Tour. The Nike Tour or the NCAA Tournament, for that matter, are full of players who can outdrive him. But he is an excellent putter, an accurate iron player, and a deft wedge player. Those are skills that assure him of making the cut in nearly all the tournaments he enters. When he's putting particularly well, he's a threat to win.

And nowadays, when he can win, he does. He won at New Orleans in 1990 by holing a bunker shot on the eighteenth hole to edge Greg Norman. He won the World Series of Golf in 1989 in a playoff against Ben Crenshaw. He's won other tournaments by building an early lead and then steadily pulling away.

But it wasn't always this way for Frosty. In his early years on the tour, he finished second eight times before he finally won. He lost playoffs. He blew putts. He got the shakes.

Frosty had to learn to close, to handle pressure. So do most golfers.

HIS GOLF CAREER began at the age of fourteen in his native South Africa, where his father owned a vineyard near Cape Town. Frosty and his brother started caddying for their father on weekend afternoons at the Stellenbosch Golf Club. When the old man was done, he'd head for the grill with his friends. Frosty and his brother would take his clubs and play until darkness fell.

Frosty liked the game and had an evident talent, particularly for putting. He took the first forty dollars he earned as a caddie and bought a mixed bag of used clubs: an old Bullseye putter, some irons, and a ladies' $1\frac{1}{2}$ wood.

He took no lessons, apart from a few clinics conducted by the South African Golf Foundation, where kids learned the rudiments of a proper stance and grip.

He just played and practiced a lot, working particularly on his short game. At school, he didn't always have time or opportunity to get to a course to practice. So he'd take some balls, a 7-iron, and an old tire, set the tire upright in some grass, and practice chipping through it. At home, his father brought a truckload of beach sand up to the farm and made a practice bunker out of it.

He played in junior tournaments during school vacations. But there was very little parental pressure to compete. Frosty feels, and I agree, that this helped him. Parents who prod a child to compete and win before he's ready can instill in the child a dread of close competition and pressure situations that carries over into adult life.

Instead, Frosty's father gave him a natural incentive. If he broke 80, his father would buy him a new set of clubs. By the time he was sixteen, Frosty was coming close.

One day, he and his father and the Stellenbosch pro played a round. After sixteen holes, Frosty needed only two pars to shoot 78.

He started thinking of the score. His swing got tense. He bogeyed the seventeenth and double-bogeyed the eighteenth.

It was his first experience with pressure, and he had failed to handle it well.

Yet Frosty chose not to think badly of himself. He decided that while he hadn't broken 80 that day, it would inevitably happen sooner or later.

Frosty attributes this attitude to a naturally optimistic personality. I'm not so sure I would call it natural.

People choose their attitudes. He could have chosen to think of himself as a choker, to believe that he would always tense up and perform poorly under pressure. He didn't. He chose to think that with experience he would get used to the pressure.

That kind of attitude makes an enormous difference in how people respond to the setbacks, disappointments, and wretched performances that inevitably attend the game of golf.

His next opportunity came at a course called Clovelly, in a junior tournament. He shot 38 on the front and thought to himself, *This is easy. I've been here before.* He brought the round home in 38 for a 76. He and his father went straight from the course to a sporting goods store, where he picked out his promised set of clubs.

Over the next two years, he brought his handicap down to one. When he had done that, he took his first personal golf lesson, from a Johannesburg pro named Phil Ritson. Shortly after, he got to scratch, and then below scratch, to plus one. He was one of the top amateurs in South Africa.

David has often mentioned to me that he became a scratch golfer, or nearly so, before he took his first formal lesson. It's an important part of his golfing personality.

He has always intuitively appreciated the fact that it's more important to learn to score than it is to learn to swing. As a boy, he learned first how to get the ball in the hole. He developed creativity and imagination, especially around the green. Then he decided it was time to clean up his swing.

In taking lessons, he's always let his feelings guide him. He might hear eight or ten different bits of advice in the course of an hour's instruction. He's always had enough confidence to nod his head in agreement on all of them while internally saying "No, that's not for me" on most of them. He'll leave a lesson with one or two things he wants to work on. After a couple of days of practice, he will boil those two things down to one glimmering feeling he tries to incorporate into his game. He's the opposite of the player who leaves a lesson trying to incorporate ten changes into his game, and after a few days of practice has expanded those ten things into a couple of dozen new moves. That kind of player hasn't got a chance on the golf course. Frosty's kind of player always has a swing he can play and score with.

I've told Frosty that it's important to take the same selective attitude toward the mental tips I give him. Some of what I teach he has always done well. He doesn't have to pay much attention to it. Some of what I teach may not feel quite right to him. In that case, he feels free to reject it or modify it. A golfer has to know himself well enough to know what is going to work for him under pressure.

Frosty had to do two years of uniformed service, and he did them in the police force, where he walked a beat and served as a court orderly. When he finished with that, he got a job as a marketing representative for a cigarette company. He played golf on his weekends, squeezing seventy-two holes of tournament play into two days of thirty-six holes each.

Again, this differed from the environment in which most American golfers develop today. Typically, the best juniors get college scholarships. The best college players immediately turn professional. They never experience the discipline of earning a living outside of golf the way that American players of earlier generations did.

Frosty feels this, too, made him a better competitor. He knows what it's like to survive on a junior cop's pay; he's done it. He knows that his life wouldn't end if his golf career did.

In fact, he didn't aspire to play professionally until he was twenty-two. He might have remained a top-flight amateur had not the South African golf authorities chosen to leave him off the national team for a test match against Taiwan. Miffed, he turned pro.

In the Southern Hemisphere summer of 1981–82, he played South Africa's December-to-February tour. He earned $16,000. He decided to try his luck in the United States.

Using his $16,000 in winnings, he flew to the United States and signed up to play one of the Florida mini-tours. But he had recently taken another swing lesson and didn't play well. He spent $5,000 on entry fees and didn't make a dime.

Again, Frosty chose to see this experience positively. He wrote off his bad play as the result of his swing change and went on to Europe's summer circuit.

He qualified for a few tournaments and won a few modest checks in Europe and returned to South Africa. He finished third on the South African Order of Merit that season, and that won him an exemption to play in Europe in 1983.

He got his first good chance to win in Europe in the summer of 1984, at a tournament in Leeds. He had the lead after the third round; he was paired Sunday with Nick Faldo. But after Saturday's play, he stopped into a golf shop and saw a 3-wood that caught his fancy. He bought it and put it into his bag the next day.

The 3-wood's shaft was much too stiff for Frosty, but back then he knew almost nothing about club specifications. He pulled the club out on the second hole and whipped a shot out-of-bounds. He finished the day with an 80.

Characteristically, though, he refused to be traumatized. He simply decided that he would never again stick a new club in his bag without understanding its specifications and testing it thoroughly.

In the fall of that year, he came to the United States to try to qualify for the PGA Tour. It was a big gamble; the plane fares and entry fees as he shuttled back and forth for the two stages of qualifying school ate up most of his bank account. But he shot a 68 in the final round and got his card.

The next spring, at the Houston Open, he had his first chance to win in the United States. Frosty was in the penultimate group, a couple of strokes behind the leader, Ray Floyd. He was also just about broke; the expense of buying a new car had wiped out his savings.

The eighteenth at the TPC at the Woodlands course is a tough finishing hole, a 445-yard par four that bends gently to the right around a lake that extends virtually from tee to green. The Sunday pin position, of course, is on the right side of the green, bringing the water dramatically into play.

After driving into the fairway on the eighteenth hole, Frosty chose to be bold. He hit a beautiful 3-iron, slightly cut, that landed on the green and stopped about six feet from the pin.

As he walked toward the green, the possibility of winning reached up and grabbed him. As a foreigner, Frosty felt keenly the importance of winning in America. It was, in his estimation, the ultimate proving ground.

The pressure was such that he felt he could barely stand. For the first time in his life, he felt his hands shaking. He thought he could see his putter fluttering and jerking in his hands like a fish on a dock. When he drew the club back, he felt no flow, no connection between his hands, the putter, and the ball. He missed the putt.

As it turned out, the putt would probably have put him into a playoff, because Floyd bogeyed the eighteenth and still won.

Golfers often ask me a variant of the chicken-and-egg question:

Which comes first, confidence or winning? The implication, in some minds, is that you can't win until you have confidence, and you can't get confidence until you've won. But if that were the case, no one would ever win for the first time. The fact is that the confidence required to win can be learned.

Frosty started learning. He chose to see the bright side of what had happened in Houston. He had hit a great 3-iron under pressure. He'd made $40,000 for finishing second, which eased his money worries. He had not accomplished everything he wanted, but he decided that the next time, he would be better prepared to cope with his nerves.

At about this time, Frosty came to see me. He had been working on his swing with David Leadbetter, and David felt that Frosty needed some help with his mental game to make sure that he got the most from his talent.

So at Leadbetter's recommendation, Frosty flew to Charlottesville to see me. We talked about some concepts that were new to him that would help him produce his best golf under pressure. They will, by this time, be familiar to you.

He had never had a consistent mental routine. Nor had he

learned the importance of focusing on a small target before each shot. We worked on incorporating both into his game.

We talked about the importance of relaxing between shots. Frosty didn't need to try to concentrate for five consecutive hours every time he played a tournament round. I encouraged him to think of other things while he waited between holes or walked after his ball. He learned to bring his attention back to golf each time he started his pre-shot routine.

We also talked about the importance of regular rest. Being so close to the edge financially and being away from home, Frosty tended to play a lot of tournaments. And he practiced a lot. I had to get him to understand that as he became better and better it was going to become more important to take time off, to stay fresh. Absence makes the heart grow fonder. When you've been away from the one you love for a while, you're twice as glad to see her when you come home. A professional player may love the game, but he has got to get away from it regularly if he wants to be excited and ready to play every time he tees off on Thursday morning.

IT WOULD BE nice to report that immediately after he started working with me, Frosty started to win. But he still had many trials to endure.

In 1987, he tied for the Western Open title with Tom Kite, Nick Price, and Fred Couples. The playoff began on the sixteenth hole. Frosty drove into the fairway. The flag was tucked to the right, next to a bunker. Frosty followed his game plan, which called for him to aim for the center of the green in that circumstance. He did, and hit his approach accurately.

Tom Kite, though, aimed for the pin and made birdie. He won the tournament.

Frosty learned from that experience. He decided that in a sudden-death playoff, he had to be more aggressive.

That same summer, in the British Open at Muirfield, he learned another lesson. He started the final round one shot off the lead, paired with Paul Azinger in the final twosome. Azinger made a couple of birdies on the first four holes.

Frosty thereupon forgot that there was much more golf to play. He decided he had to chase Azinger. He got too aggressive with his birdie putts and ran several of them far enough by the hole that he three-putted. He fell out of contention.

Ironically, it was Nick Faldo who won that day, making pars on every hole. Azinger came back to him. He would have come back to Frosty too, had Frosty been more patient.

That's all part of learning to win at the highest level. A golfer has to have a finely honed sense of when to be aggressive and when to be patient.

Frosty's sense of it required just a little more honing. The next spring, he was at Hilton Head, playing well in the MCI Classic. He was in Sunday's last group, and he held the lead briefly around the turn. But he bogeyed the twelfth hole, and Greg Norman overtook him.

Down the stretch, Frosty hit every green and missed every birdie putt. He wound up losing to Norman in a playoff.

He decided after that that he'd been too anxious to sink those birdie putts. He needs to be just a bit indifferent and nonchalant to hit them as well as he can. He adopted a new thought for his putting routine: *It doesn't matter.* It relaxed him.

We talked a lot by phone on Sunday evenings during those years. I always tried to remind Frosty that although he might not have won, he'd played solid rounds. He'd proven he knew how to win, knew how to handle his mind and emotions. Someone else had happened to have a great day. Even so, he'd learned from it. We were able to take near misses and turn them into something positive.

He was ready to win.

At the Southern Open later in 1988, Frosty had a two-shot lead at one point on the back nine. But he three-putted the fourteenth and sixteenth holes to fall one behind Bob Tway.

The final hole was a long par five, downhill, with a stream that cut across the fairway about thirty yards in front of the green. Frosty hit a good drive, but he was still too far to reach the green.

He thought he could, however, get over the stream and leave himself with a short little chip to set up a birdie. It was a risky, aggressive shot, but he played it well. His pitch, though, was about eight feet short of the pin.

He slammed the club into the ground. But it was not, as some spectators surmised, because he was displeased with his pitch. He was pumping himself up to make his birdie putt.

Frosty walked onto the green. This time, there were no tremors. This time, he had a routine that was focused solely on putting the ball into the hole. This time, he made the putt. And he won the playoff.

It had taken three years and seven second-place finishes for Frosty to develop from the golfer with the shaking hands who missed a crucial six-footer and lost at Houston into the confident, aggressive golfer who shrugged off his mistakes and won the Southern Open by sinking a crucial eight-footer.

Frosty managed this because he chose to believe that each loss was a beneficial experience. He drew the lessons he could from them and then forgot about them. That's the way any golfer should approach a loss.

It's not what happens to golfers, but how they choose to respond to what happens that distinguishes champions.

Since the Southern Open, he's won eight more tournaments in the United States and several others in South Africa. He continues to learn how to close.

At the 1989 World Series of Golf, he hit a bad 7-iron approach to the eighteenth green in the final round, pulling the ball into the gallery area and leaving himself an awkward chip from a sidehill lie.

But he realized, as he walked toward the green, what he had done wrong. He had stood too long over the 7-iron, trying to be too fine with it. He should have stuck to his routine, stepped up to the ball, and swung without delay. Delay, he realized, only made his muscles tense.

He returned to his routine for the chip shot, hit it stiff, and went on to take the title in the playoff.

He still feels nervous in tight situations. But he doesn't let his nerves overcome him as he did earlier in his career. At the 1990 Million Dollar Challenge in Sun City, South Africa, he took his second straight title with a birdie on the eighteenth green that defeated Jose Maria Olazabal. He putted it with shaking hands.

Occasionally, he doesn't close well. In 1994, at Phoenix, he had the lead with ten holes to play, when he hit a bad shot and lapsed into trying to fix his mechanics. He shot 42 for the back nine.

And there are still situations he has yet to conquer. He's never won a major championship. That's a level of pressure that the professionals can feel only four times a year. It may take him longer to learn how to deal with it.

But, as ever, he learns and goes on.

No. 14

How Guy Rotella Came to Golf

WHEN I VISIT WITH MY FATHER, GUY, WE TALK SOMETIMES ABOUT the golfers I've met. I remember telling him once about something said during the course of a day I spent with Ben Hogan. I had asked Hogan what his adolescence was like.

"I never had an adolescence," Ben replied.

The bleakness of that response stuck with me, and I was curious to know my Dad's reaction.

"Well, I didn't have an adolescence either," Dad said.

That startled me, because I had never once heard my father, who was then seventy-six, complain about his life.

He had, he explained, never thought there was anything to complain about. His generation had a different understanding of adolescence. The average teenager in his time and place worked, studied, went to sleep. He didn't think he had an inalienable right to play sports, to go to parties. Anything of that sort was a windfall.

My dad was born in 1919, in Rutland, Vermont, one of eight children. My grandfather worked at the Rutland Marble Finishing Plant. Weekends he worked a second job, chopping trees and selling firewood so he could pay down the mortgage on the family house.

When my father was nine, my grandfather was promoted to yard foreman at the marble plant. Shortly thereafter, he was in the yard supervising the movement of some heavy marble blocks, when one of them fell from the crane and crushed him, killing him instantly.

My grandmother was left with eight kids and a mortgage-free house. There was no Social Security or workmen's compensation back then. Somehow, she made do. She took in boarders. Every night after dinner, she and her daughters would do finishing work on belts from a Rutland garment factory. She had a chicken coop and a garden.

And she got help from the community. Every autumn, men who had come from my grandfather's village in Sicily would go out into the woods and bring back enough firewood to keep the Rotella family warm through the winter. In the spring, they would come with shovels and spades and work the garden soil so the family could plant vegetables.

Another friend of my grandfather called and said, "Send the boy to my barber shop and we'll look after him." And that was how my father learned the trade that sustained him for much of his life.

He continued going to school, to Mount St. Joseph's Academy, where my brothers, sisters, and I would eventually go. He cut hair and he studied. At nine o'clock each night, my grandmother would take the fuse out of the fuse box so he would have to stop reading and go to sleep. She was worried about the electric bill.

After high school, he bought a barber shop, and he ran that for two years until he had saved enough money to enroll at the University of Alabama, where tuition was only thirty dollars per semester and a room was a dollar a week. He was there until 1941, when the war broke out. He went into the Navy, and then he met my mother. They married and started a family, and that was the end of his formal education, though he never stopped reading and learning. He and my mother helped put five kids through college, three of them through graduate school.

I recount all this partly because I admire what my father has achieved, and partly to explain why he came late to golf.

Dad was sixty-three when I persuaded him and my mother to try golf. Until that time, they had never set foot on the grounds of the Rutland Country Club. But I believe that you're never too old to learn to play golf, as long as you're not afraid to try. And I had never seen my father fail to accomplish something he set his mind to doing—gardening, plumbing, or any other chore around the house. I remember he once built a stereo receiver out of what seemed to me to be a million tiny pieces. All he needs to do is see a way to reach a goal. Then he'll get there.

It took a while for them to see the goal. They took no lessons, and for the first few months, they played mainly with each other. But within a year, they both loved the game. My mother had a rhythmic, repeatable swing from the start. Dad read everything he could get his hands on about the game. He discovered that he had a good natural putting touch. And when he realized he was good enough to play with his brother and some of his other lifelong friends, he was like a kid with a new toy.

His first year, he scored in triple digits. Over the next ten years or so, he brought that score down slowly and steadily.

His progress came to an abrupt halt three years ago. He was playing in a tournament, and his shoulder was sore from a fall he'd taken. Someone he was playing with suggested that he could loosen the shoulder up by windmilling it. Dad tried it.

Never accept free medical advice from somebody you meet on the golf course.

Dad tore his rotator cuff apart. The likelihood is it already was damaged, perhaps from the years he spent with his arm extended, cutting hair. But windmilling completed the process. He couldn't raise his left arm.

He waited for a couple of months to see if it would get better with rest. It didn't. He needed surgery. Just before he went under, he told the surgeon to make certain he left a golf swing somewhere in that shoulder. But when the operation was over, the doctors told my mother that they couldn't predict the range of motion my father would regain.

There were people my father's age in Rutland who had undergone rotator cuff surgery and hadn't regained full use of their shoulders. He chose to assume that they were disabled because they hadn't done their rehabilitation exercises. He was going to do his exercises. He wanted to play golf again. He understood that a person is never too old to improve his physical condition, never too old to dream and improve. Golf had become the new challenge and the new toy of his retirement, and he was not about to give it up.

Three times every day, he did those exercises. At first, the effort exhausted him so much that all he could do afterwards was sit and rest until it was time to do them again. Gradually, he got stronger. One day he walked into his surgeons' office and raised his arm over his head. They were as excited and surprised as kids at the circus to see how well he was doing.

A few months after the surgery, I was home for a visit and he drove me to the airport in Burlington. There was an indoor driving range nearby, and I asked him to stop there. He wasn't supposed to be doing anything athletic that early, but I gave him a 7-iron and put a ball on a tee and told him to hit it with a three-quarter swing. He did. Then he hit one with a smooth, full swing. He said it felt fine.

"That's enough for now," I said. "Use this as fuel for motivation to keep working on those exercises. You're going to play golf again."

He continued to work hard on his rehabilitation, and still does. By the next spring he was playing and improving once more. That's one of the great things about golf. Until the end of a person's life, it affords pleasure, exercise, and goals to work toward.

Dad's goal became breaking 80. He's still working on it.

In his case, the mental nature of the barrier was evident when he played his best round to date at Rutland. He was out with his regular group: Frank Esposito, Sal Salerni, and my uncle Roy. They're compatible players. Uncle Roy carries a 13 handicap, my dad's an 18, and Frank and Sal are somewhere in that region as well, although my dad tells me that Sal's game has slipped a bit since he started spending a lot of his spare time on flying lessons. They usually play a two-dollar Nassau, with a little extra money for birdies and greenies.

It was July, the peak of the golf season in Vermont. People have played enough to get their swings grooved. It's warm enough to get the muscles loose.

Rutland Country Club is a beautiful, tight old course, not very long. The greens are slick bent grass, among the finest anywhere. It's a course that demands accuracy and good putting.

Fortunately, those are Dad's strong suits. He's not very long, maybe 180 yards with the driver. But he's usually in the fairway. And he's a confident putter.

On this particular day, Dad felt great. The weather was good and everyone was happy. It was one of those days, he recalled later, when the shots don't take any effort. Everything feels smooth. He was picking out small targets and thinking about making the ball go there. That was all he was thinking about, save for a general feeling that it was good to be alive and playing golf on such a glorious day with three good friends.

He parred the first, then got up and down from off the green to par the second. He kept making pars or bogeys until the front nine was done. Then it happened.

"Geez, Rotella," Sal said. "You shot a 39!"

At that moment, Dad's thinking snapped out of the present. He stopped thinking about the next shot and started thinking that he could break 80.

He started thinking he was on a hot streak, which wasn't exactly true. He was simply playing up to his potential. Thinking *I'm on a hot streak* can be harmful if the subconscious corollary is *I'm bound to cool off.*

Sal's announcement that Dad had shot 39 was the equivalent of those people at the PGA Championship screaming "Ryder Cup!" at Brad Faxon.

Just as Brad had to keep the Ryder Cup out of his mind, Dad had to keep breaking 80 out of his.

Ideally, no one would add up his score and no one would think about it until the round was over. But in the real world, lots of people are going to keep track of your score, if only to figure out who won the two-dollars for the front side. And lots of people can't seem to avoid adding it up for themselves, even if they're playing alone.

Those people have to treat the knowledge of a partial score the same way Brad treated those cries of "Ryder Cup!"—as a stimulus to keeping their minds in the present and thinking about their routines.

Dad didn't quite manage this. He hit his approach into a trap on No. 10 and couldn't get up and down. He bogeyed the next three holes, although on a couple of them he could have saved par with some good wedge play.

By that time, he was thinking that he was in danger of blowing his good start.

I find this a common problem with players trying hard, perhaps too hard, to put together a great round or a great tournament. Sometimes I ask them what their attitudes would be if I told them that I had just been visited with a divine revelation. It was already written in heaven that they were going to win three times this year on the tour, or break 80, or whatever their goals might be.

Guaranteed.

In the bag.

All they had to do was enjoy watching it happen.

If that were true, they all would be a lot more patient, a lot more accepting. If they hit a bad shot, their attitude would be, "Wow! I hit it into the gunch on this hole and I'm still going to win! What a great story this is going to make!"

If they had that attitude, they'd win or break 80 a lot more often.

But Dad got a little anxious and went for the green with his second shot at No. 14, hitting a 3-wood. That's a hole he normally lays up on.

He missed with the 3-wood, and then went into what he might call his Jimmy Piersall syndrome. He gave up on the hole, got angry, wedged badly, and made a double-bogey.

This is proof enough that golf is a confounding and intriguing sport. My dad is a tough man. When he was in the Navy, he won boxing and wrestling championships. Golf is the only thing I've ever seen that can grab his emotions, excite him, and shake his composure that way.

He finished with 44, for an 83. It was an excellent round for an 18-handicapper, but it could have been better. It could have been under 80. It was a near miss.

Of course, my Dad's miss was leavened by the fact that whatever happens on the course, he walks off the last green pleased that he had a chance to play. That's a great thing. It's one reason I'm confident he will make it into the 70s sometime soon, so long as he remembers to stay in the present. I'm thrilled that he has the game, and proud that I introduced him to it.

I WISH THAT I set a better playing example for Dad. But staying in the present can be much harder to do than it is to say.

I played with him recently in the Member-Guest Tournament at Rutland, a four-ball, best-ball event. We were even going into the eighteenth hole in our semifinal match. No. 18 at Rutland is a long par four, a dogleg left with a tee shot over water.

We seemed to be in good shape to win. I reached the green in two, though I left myself a downhill, sidehill putt of maybe sixty feet. Dad was just off the green in three. Our opponents looked out of it. One of them had picked up. The other was over the green in three, facing a pitch to a green that sloped severely from back to front. It looked as if either of us could win the hole—Dad by getting up and down, me by two- or even three-putting.

This was when I stopped thinking about the present and started thinking about the future. I thought about how neat it would be for Dad to make the putt that won the match. He'd been playing well that day. I thought about how pleased he would be.

Dad chipped up for his fourth shot, and it stopped about five feet below the hole, the kind of putt he usually handles well. Our opponent hit his fourth shot. He caught the ball very thin and hit a low line drive. It looked like it would certainly fly over the front of the green and make our situation even easier. But it hit the flag stick and stopped an inch from the hole. We conceded his putt for a five.

Suddenly, I had to try to jerk my thoughts back into the present. I couldn't quite do it. I left my first putt about six feet short. I missed the second. Dad missed.

We lost the playoff.

I thought, *Great. I spend my days teaching people to stay in the present. But today I don't do it myself.*

That's part of the challenge of the game. It's not enough to learn what to do. You need the discipline to make yourself do it every day.

Fortunately, every new day is a fresh chance. So I'm hopeful that Dad will invite me back to the Member-Guest. If he does, I plan to redeem myself.

No. 15

How Nona Epps Learned to Come

Through in the Clutch

IT SOMETIMES SEEMS TO ME THAT THERE ARE BUT TWO KINDS OF parents: those who want their kids to play golf, and those who want their kids to play golf better.

Some parents seek me out because they have kids who don't seem interested in the sport, which the parents love. Understandably, the parents want to pass along to their children the pleasures and benefits of their game.

Others have kids who started playing the game, showed some ability, and then abruptly decided to give it up.

Still others have kids who have truly promising games: They've won the junior club championship, or something on the high school level, and now these parents can see college scholarships and maybe a professional career ahead, if only the child would just apply herself.

I'm tempted to refer all of these parents to a friend of mine named Charlie Epps, because Charlie is a proven expert in raising a young golfer the right way.

We got to know each other as colleagues. Charlie is a teaching pro from Houston, but he has done a lot of work for *Golf Digest* schools where I've been on the staff. Charlie loves the game and is an excellent player as well as a teacher. He believes firmly in the importance of a golfer's attitude, and we spent a lot of dinners chewing over ideas on the best ways to think about golf.

He had a personal as well as a professional interest in the subject, for he had two daughters, Nona and Mimi. Over the years, he's asked me a lot of questions about kids, parents, and golf.

He wanted to instill in his girls a love for the game and a confident attitude that would help them maximize whatever talent they have.

To start with, Charlie understood two key principles. One is that no parent is going to make a kid like golf. And the second is that it will do no good to restrict a child to golf at the expense of other sports.

The best way to introduce a kid to golf is casually.

Let him come out to the course with you once in a while, preferably late in the day when it's not so crowded. Let him drive the cart. Around the greens, give him a ball and a chipping club and a putter. Most kids instinctively understand the notion of putting a ball into a hole.

Remember that the child's attention span will be short, probably way too short for an eighteen-hole round. A parent has to recognize that the first objective in taking the child to the course is for the child to have fun. When the child stops having fun, it's time to go home.

In short, let the child dictate the nature and duration of the experience. If the kid wants to walk, don't take a cart—or vice versa. If the child wants to drop a ball in a bunker just to see what hitting it out of there feels like, let him. If he wants to take time out to see if there are tadpoles in the creek by the third fairway, that's fine too. If he wants to quit and go swimming after five holes, quit and go swimming.

This means that the parent has to recognize that his or her own game has a lesser priority when a child is along. If you're determined to get in eighteen holes or if you're interested in shooting your best score, leave the child somewhere else.

Too often, I see or hear about parents who do just the opposite. They take the child to the course, walk onto the first tee, hand him or her a driver, and expect the kid to hit the ball with it. When the child dribbles the ball off the tee, the parent counts, "one." And the parent then makes the child endure this for another five hours, until a proper round has been played.

Or I see parents who give the child no reason to think that golf is enjoyable. They moan and groan—or worse—when one of their shots is less than perfect. Why would a child want to play a game that demonstrably makes his father or mother unhappy, frustrated, and angry?

On the other hand, what kid wouldn't want to play a game if he sees that players celebrate their good shots and laugh off the bad ones?

Some parents want to play Joe Expert with the kid, constantly correcting his swing. Especially in the early stages, I think this is a mistake. No kid wants to spend hours being lectured and corrected. Let the child learn by imitation for a while. Let her swing however she wants to swing.

There is, of course, one exception to the rule of letting the child do what he wants and have fun. And that concerns etiquette. Any child who wants to throw clubs or other sorts of tantrums should be immediately and firmly set straight. Generally, though, that shouldn't happen if the child isn't kept out on the course longer than he or she wants to be.

A little farther down the road, you might want to teach a child a sound grip. And a little beyond that, it might be time for lessons. I think group lessons are best, particularly if they lead to a child's playing and competing against other children.

This was the basic approach Charlie Epps took with his older daughter, Nona. Since he was a teaching pro, she was always around golf courses. As a youngster, she'd occasionally go out with her dad because she liked to drive the cart. And she took group lessons with other kids.

But though she was the daughter of a pro, Nona Epps never played a full eighteen-hole round of golf until she was a freshman in high school.

She played volleyball and softball and ran track most of the year. Charlie encouraged her to do it. He let her know that whatever sport she wanted to play was fine with him. Golf was available, but only to the extent she wanted it.

She started to take to the game when she entered high school and found that her school had a golf team. She liked being part of a team. She liked competing.

At this point, Charlie started to become more active with her. He made sure she had good mechanical fundamentals—the grip, the stance, the swing. The important thing was that he taught them to her when she was ready to learn them, instead of trying to force them on her when he, not she, was ready.

And he always remembered the importance of helping her develop a good attitude and a good mental game.

He and Nona started sharing what Charlie called "positive notes." When she played in a high school event, he'd give her a small piece of paper to carry in her pocket. It might say "Smile. Relax. Play in the present. Have fun. No omars."

An "omar" is the Epps's code word for a mental mistake like forgetting your routine.

And she'd prepare notes for him when he played. She might write "Good grip. Good stance. Good swing," on a piece of paper that he'd carry.

It's great if a parent can recognize that communication with a child is a two-way process. I like it when parents let kids give them advice on things like reading putts. I think parents would be amazed at how much they could learn if they let themselves see the game through the imaginative eyes of a child once in a while. Most important, it helps in building a good, amicable relationship with the child.

IN NONA'S FRESHMAN season, she made good progress. Her first competitive round was about 123. By the end of the spring, she broke 100 for the first time, winning a fifty-dollar prize from her grandparents.

At this point, her interest in golf shouldered aside her other athletic pursuits. She started playing golf year round.

When this happens with a child, it's great, as long as the desire comes from the child, not the parent.

A child of almost any age can't spend too much time playing golf and practicing. But children burn out if they're doing it because someone requires it and they're not having fun.

At this stage in his kids' development, Charlie and his wife started taking the girls to the golf course for a regular Sunday round. They'd invent small competitions for Nona and Mimi: who could chip closest, who could drive farthest.

Charlie started to be a little more demanding of Nona. He'd show her a shot and expect that she'd work at it on the range. He might even let a little frustration show if she didn't.

But he didn't push her too far or too fast. At the high school age, a lot of parents want their children to enter national competitions. For one thing, they know that college golf coaches scout those competitions and hand out scholarships to children who do well in them.

There's even a certain amount of reverse sandbagging that goes on. The USGA, for instance, might say that only girls with handicaps of five or less can enter a certain event. Some parents will do what they can to finagle their children's handicaps under the limit or get them a waiver.

Charlie didn't do that. Nona never played in the USGA junior competitions.

I think that's a sound idea. Boxing managers, it seems to me, have always had a wise strategy for bringing along a promising young fighter. They don't overmatch him. In fact, they lean over backwards to give him easy opposition. They let him pile up a lot of wins against tomato cans, building confidence, before they ask him to step in against anyone remotely comparable in ability.

Young golfers can benefit from the same kind of easy early competition. I think a boy or girl is a lot better off winning local tournaments than losing badly at the national level. Losing is no fun for a lot of kids. It's a proximate cause of burnout. There'll be time enough later on to learn that it's a competitive world and no one wins all the time.

In her sophomore season, Nona did something quite remarkable. She was scoring consistently in the 90s, until one day she shot 80. She improved her previous best score by better than ten strokes.

This tells me a lot about the attitudes Charlie taught her.

First, he taught her to play in the present. She didn't know how many strokes she was taking until she added them up at the end of the round.

Thus, she had no comfort level to break through. When a golfer has been playing for a while, he can start thinking of himself as a 90s shooter, or an 80s shooter. If he starts to play significantly better than that, and fails to keep his mind focused tightly in the present, he can become distracted by his own score, perhaps by a feeling that he's playing over his head and is bound to come back to his "normal" level, his comfort level.

Nona didn't have that problem. When she found herself playing well, she just continued to play well.

Not only that. Charlie never emphasized scores with her. He certainly never let his attitude toward Nona be affected by the scores she posted. She knew that whether she shot 80 or 180, he would still ask only whether she had fun and whether she stayed committed to her routine.

The next year, Nona broke 80 for the first time in competition, shooting 78. She still wasn't consistent, but she started to emerge as one of the better girls in Texas high school golf. Her scoring average was in the low 80s, and she had the occasional 74 or 73.

Golf was by no means the only priority in her life. Nona wanted to go to Texas Christian University, and that is where she went, even though she wasn't offered a golf scholarship. She got some letters from smaller schools interested in recruiting her for their golf teams, but they didn't interest her. That was fine with Charlie. He didn't particularly want her to have the pressure of justifying a golf scholarship.

Nona didn't even play golf in her freshman year at TCU. She wanted to get acclimated to university academics. She wanted to join a sorority and have some fun. She did those things.

At the beginning of her sophomore year, she tried out for, and made, the golf team. Then she faced a four-round qualifying competition for girls who wanted to make the traveling squad that was headed to a big intercollegiate event in Nebraska.

Nona shot 77 and led the field after the first day. She followed that with a 79. But in the third round, she ballooned to an 88. Her chance of making the traveling team suddenly seemed remote.

When she called home after shooting 88, Charlie just said, "Go get 'em tomorrow."

The TCU women played the final qualifying round at Mira Vista Golf Club, a tough new Tom Weiskopf–Jay Morrish design outside Fort Worth.

Nona hit a 3-wood and a 5-iron to the fringe of the first green. She sank the long putt and felt a surge of confidence. She followed that with another birdie putt on the third hole. She was trusting her putting stroke. She saw a line and she hit the ball.

On No. 4, she hit to eight feet, giving herself another birdie putt, one that would have put her three under par. "Take 'em when you can get 'em," she remembered her father saying. Then another thought entered her mind: *I'm two under. Maybe I've used up my supply of birdies.*

With that in mind, she missed that putt. Then she did a smart thing. She chastised herself for letting her mental routine break down on the birdie putt, for hitting it while in doubt. And she resolved not to repeat that mistake.

She had a bogey and a birdie the rest of the way out and made the turn at two-under 32; par for the front side was 34, since one par four had a temporary green and was being played as a par three.

It was the first time she had ever played nine holes under par. But she put that idea out of her mind and drove well on the downhill tenth, a 363-yard par four. She had a 9-iron into the green.

Nona went through her routine. She stood behind the ball, visualizing her shot. Then she tugged on the bill of her visor. She looked at her target and found an intermediate target on the same line, a few feet in front of her ball. She put the club in her right hand, aligned it, and took her stance and grip.

And at that point, she had a little epiphany. She remembered once playing a round with Charlie, and she could almost hear again something he had said when she executed a similar down-hill pitch: "I'm impressed with the way you play that shot."

With that compliment from her father in mind, she swung and lofted the ball into the air. It hit a foot from the pin and stuck.

Parents, I think, would be amazed at how often something they've said will pop into their children's brains at a critical moment. If they knew how often this happened, they might take care to improve the odds that it would be something positive and helpful.

Nona made her putt and she was three under. She picked up another birdie at No. 11, then bogeyed the thirteenth, a very long, tough par four. She pitched in from seventy yards and eagled the fourteenth.

Two holes later, her round was interrupted. By prearrangement, Nona had to drive a teammate back to the TCU campus for a late class.

A lot of golfers would have used this as an excuse to play badly for the remaining two holes. They would have dwelt on how unfortunate they were to have such a great round broken up, right on the verge of breaking 70.

Nona didn't. She played rhythm and blues on the car radio as she drove back and forth to the campus, thinking that this would help her maintain the good rhythm she had going that day. As darkness neared, she drove back out to the course and finished up clean.

In the first critical round of her college career, she broke par for the first time in her life. She broke 70 for the first time in her life. She shot 65.

As I said, her Dad raised her not to know comfort levels.

• • •

OF COURSE, ONE round does not a career make. Nona made the TCU traveling squad and went to Nebraska for the tournament. The weather was cold, and so was she. She couldn't break 80. She still has a lot to learn about consistency and playing in adverse conditions.

The next challenge she'll face is keeping her loose, optimistic attitude even if she makes a true commitment to see how good she can get at golf. It's relatively easy to stay positive if golf is something you regard as a hobby. If it becomes your main work or passion in life, it gets harder to smile at bad bounces and stubbed chips.

But she and her father have built a great foundation.

No. 16

How Pat Bradley

Finished Her Victory Lap

···
···
···

THE MOST INTENSE ATHLETE WITH WHOM I HAVE EVER WORKED MIGHT not draw a second glance walking through the average shopping mall.

Our media stereotype of the intense, mentally tough athlete is a masculine one—maybe a linebacker, shot full of pain killers, laying waste to quarterbacks on Sunday afternoon. Not many sportswriters associate intensity and toughness with the image of a slightly built woman, prematurely gray, with a shy, unassuming demeanor. But mental toughness has no gender. Pat Bradley is slightly built, shy, and unassuming. But Pat has an intensity that can sear you when she chooses to reveal it. She is as mentally tough as any human being I have ever known.

When Pat first came to see me, she had been a fixture on the LPGA Tour for about ten years. She'd already won a number of tournaments, including the U.S. Women's Open. But it was what she had to say about herself that impressed me.

She didn't want to talk about the tournaments she'd won. She wanted to talk about the times she'd finished second. She wanted to know how she could convert those second place finishes into firsts. She understood that no matter how good a player is, she faces two choices. She can get better. Or she can stagnate.

And Pat wanted to get better, because she had great dreams and huge ambitions. She wanted to win more tournaments, especially major championships. She wanted to be Player of the Year. She wanted to be in the LPGA Hall of Fame. I love to work with athletes who dream.

What impressed me most was why Pat thought she could do such things. She had never been a prodigy, one of the USGA's golden girls. She grew up in New Hampshire and Massachusetts, the daughter of a man who owned a ski and sports shop. Golf seasons are relatively short in New England, and as a junior player she didn't rank with her peers from California and the South, who got to play all year round. She was, she likes to say, a "local yokel." It wasn't until she was halfway through college at Florida International that she thought her game might be good enough for the LPGA.

Even then she didn't have any flashy physical talent to set her apart. She drives the ball about 230 yards, which was average for the LPGA. She didn't have the silken roll that marks a great natural putter like Ben Crenshaw or Nancy Lopez.

What Pat did have was an appreciation for the power of her own mind. She felt she was capable of seeing every shot before she hit it, of willing herself to get the ball in the hole. And that kind of resolve can more than make up for a little bit less than optimal length off the tee.

Pat had already figured out most of what I teach golfers about the mental game. It was a challenge to me to find ways to help her get even better.

She mentioned that when she got into position to win, she started to feel the physical symptoms of nerves. She got butterflies. And she feared that.

I told her to embrace the butterflies. They signified that she was where she was supposed to be. She had worked hard to be good enough to get into contention. The onset of nerves only verified that her hard work was paying off.

Pat liked that idea, and she used it to help herself get comfortable either in the lead or challenging for it.

She liked another idea I mentioned to her. I told her that our bodies and brains are, in one sense at least, like computers. The data that a computer receives will inevitably be reflected in the data it puts out.

This reinforced her ability to see her shots before she hit them. She believed that she could win because she had the strongest mind, the best ability to visualize successful shots. She gave her mind only positive input.

And then she went on a tear. In 1986, she won the Dinah Shore, the LPGA, and the du Maurier. She lost the U.S. Women's Open by a few strokes. It was the closest any LPGA player has ever come to the Grand Slam. She fulfilled her dream of being Player of the Year. Then she did it again in 1991.

Pat in those years played with her eyes. No matter where she hit the ball, she thought calmly and confidently about getting the next shot where she wanted it to go. She rolled in putts from all over the green. She made par from woods, from water, from sand. It didn't matter. She saw herself as Houdini, able to escape from anything. No matter how many shots she fell behind, she believed she could come back. And with that attitude, she often could. At one 1986 tournament, with an elite field of sixteen players, she started the final round almost in last place, seven strokes off the lead. She shot 63 and won.

She had a lot in common with Ben Hogan. Neither one was a great player at the outset. They needed a long time to get to the top. Like Hogan's, Pat's discipline was so intense that she had no attention to spare for small talk. She had a reputation as a grim player, and a silent one. Of course, that was a distorted perspective. As Pat once told me, "From the time I teed off to the time I finished, I was always talking. I was in constant, silent communication with myself."

It was just that people couldn't hear it, couldn't share it.

At times in those years, I worried about how hard Pat drove herself. She couldn't leave the game at the golf course. As soon as one round was over, she started thinking about the next one, planning every shot on every hole. More often than not, she ate dinner by herself in her room. For company, she might have an occasional Red Sox or Celtics game on television.

As Pat herself will tell you, she had an intense fear of failure. She worried that if she played badly, she would be letting people down—her father, the rest of her family, even her fans. It didn't matter that the truth was that her family and friends would have felt the same about her no matter how she played. No matter how much she achieved, she was unrelentingly self-critical. If she shot 68, she was all right. If she shot 75, she was a bum—in her own mind.

I told her that she should be clapping herself on the back more often for the great things that she'd accomplished. But Pat found that very hard to do. There was no denying that her intensity was helping her win golf tournaments. And she wanted very much to win golf tournaments.

In 1987, she fell ill with Graves' disease, but she continued to whip herself to perform. Graves' disease is an illness of the thyroid gland. In Pat, it manifested itself as shaking hands, body tremors, and general weakness. On the course, she had to change her position at address, because she was afraid her shaking hands might inadvertently cause the club to move the ball. She turned away from other competitors when she took a drink of water, for fear they would see the liquid sloshing in the cup. At airports, she could barely make it up the first step into a rental car courtesy van.

But she confided in no one, fearful of showing weakness. For nearly a year, she told herself that she just needed a rest, that she was trying too hard, or even that she was creating the symptoms psychosomatically.

Finally, on a layover in Dallas in early 1988, she called a friend, Dr. Skip Garvey. He listened to her describe her symptoms for about five minutes. He ordered immediate blood tests. The next day, when he told her she was physically sick, Pat felt as happy as if she'd just won a golf tournament. At least there was something really wrong with her. At least *she* had not failed. It was just her body. And there was a cure.

Her illness demonstrated that no matter how mentally tough an athlete might be, calamity can still befall her. Toughness is not invulnerability. But toughness can help to overcome calamity. It did with Pat.

She took radiation treatment and started on a medication regimen. Gradually, she and her doctors brought the disease under control. By 1989, she started to win again. Her ultimate goal hove into view—the LPGA Hall of Fame.

The LPGA Hall of Fame is the most exclusive shrine in sports. No one is elected. To make it in, a player has to win thirty LPGA tournaments, including two majors. By way of comparison, if the same standard were in use for the men's tour, only one currently active player—Tom Watson—would have enough wins to qualify. No one else would be close.

In 1991, Pat went on another tear, winning five tournaments and Player of the Year honors again. In the autumn of that year, she won two tournaments back-to-back, for her twenty-ninth and thirtieth victories. The penultimate victory, the Safeco Classic, was an archetypal Bradley triumph. She birdied the seventy-second hole to tie Rosie Jones at 280. They went back to the tee at No. 18, a par five, for the playoff. Pat sliced her drive into a creek. She dropped, hit a wood, then a full 9-iron fourth, and sank an eighteen-foot par putt to keep the playoff going. She birdied the next hole to win. She really was like Houdini.

When she won the next week, she was in. She had nothing left to prove.

And as soon as that happened, she stopped winning.

"I was exhausted," Pat has told me. The mental effort that enabled her to win golf tournaments, the ascetic discipline, had taken a lot out of her. Making it into the Hall of Fame enabled her to tell herself she could rest.

She looked around and decided that there were other things in her life that she wanted to pay attention to. Her relationship with her fellow competitors had always been respectful, but generally distant. She started cultivating friendships, going out to dinner. She chatted a little on the golf course. She even enjoyed the faint look of shock on the other players' faces when she talked and smiled during a round.

The slight change in her personality, however, affected her golf. Putts she would have made in 1986 and 1991 lipped out in 1992 and 1993. Her confidence in her ability to get the ball in the hole wavered. Without that bright, flaming intensity, her physical skills were just average. For three seasons, she was winless, and she finished no higher than nineteenth on the money list.

I told her not to worry. She was taking the psychological equivalent of a victory lap. It's only natural that a person's desires change as her life progresses. When it was over, when she'd smelled the flowers long enough, she would know what to do to get back to winning.

A couple of years after her Hall of Fame ceremony, Pat called me up. She had decided her victory lap was over.

"This has been fun, Bob," she said. "But I don't want to drop off the earth. I don't care if I win all the time, but I want to be one of the top ten players again."

So we started talking about ways to balance an intense approach to golf with being the sunnier, friendlier golfing personality she had become since 1991. We started talking about ways she could still win, but without exhausting and isolating herself. If she could adapt, we decided, she could have it both ways.

Step one was a slightly curtailed schedule. During her best years, Pat played a lot of tournaments. Typically, she'd go on tour for six weeks in a row. And she felt she usually reached her peak in the last three weeks of that stretch.

We discussed playing no more than three consecutive weeks without a rest. The trick, I said, was to forget about using the first tournament or two to warm up. She had to be at her best from the first day of the first tournament.

We talked about learning to leave the game at the golf course. I encouraged her to keep developing friendships, to help younger players, to share what she'd learned. She would be giving something back to the game by doing so; she'd also be helping herself. She could still take a limited time each evening to think about the next day's round, visualizing her shots.

On the course, I felt she needn't spend the whole day in an isolation chamber. She could continue to talk to her fellow competitors and to the gallery and still play well if she could learn to modify her pre-shot routine. She needed to insert a step in the routine that consisted of shutting out all the outside distractions and getting into her old, intense mode of thinking. She had to learn to turn it on and turn it off.

This is an important lesson for anyone who hopes to play competitive golf and maintain a family and a social life.

A golfer has to learn to compartmentalize. The happiest players are the ones who do.

Over the last year or so, Pat has worked hard on finding this balance in her life. It is starting to pay off.

She started last season with her game in great shape after a winter of practice. She had taken to heart my advice that if she was going to play a curtailed schedule, she had to be ready to play whenever she teed it up. She could not afford, as some players do, to play her way into competitive shape.

On the practice range before that first round of the season, at the Chrysler-Plymouth Tournament of Champions at the Grand Cypress course in Orlando, Pat was hitting the ball beautifully. She was thinking, *Sound the bell! I'm ready.* She was cocky.

And she shot 79.

That night, she shed tears of frustration. Then she rallied. "Pat, there are three more days," she told herself. "You can bounce back. You've done it before."

For the next three days, she used the pain of that 79 to goad herself, and she played excellent golf. She finished the tournament tied for third.

The players stayed in Orlando for the next tournament, the HealthSouth Inaugural at Disney World's Eagle Pines Course. Pat opened with a 71 and a 72, but the course was playing very tough in cold, windy weather. She was only two shots off the lead held by Beth Daniel.

Entering the final round of the fifty-four-hole event, she felt relaxed and free of pressure. After three winless years, she thought, no one expected her to overtake Daniel. Only Pat knew how close she was to regaining the form she had had in 1986 and 1991.

She struck the ball beautifully on the front nine, hitting every fairway and every green. But the greens on the course were chewed-up Bermuda grass, and she made only one birdie putt, although she had several of about four feet and half a dozen inside fifteen feet.

Pat stayed patient. It seems almost contradictory, but during her intense, winning years, she was always able to stay patient. During her victory-lap years, when her intensity wasn't as good, she had less patience. She found herself slamming the putter back into the bag when she was unhappy with her performance on the greens.

In fact, there is no contradiction. When she was at her most intense, Pat was also her most confident. A confident player shrugs off a missed birdie putt and figures that the miss only improves the odds that the next one will go in.

That was how Pat felt that Sunday afternoon in Florida.

She birdied Nos. 11 and 12 to take the lead at four under. But Daniel, playing behind her, regrouped with birdies of her own at Nos. 14 and 15. She drew even.

Pat hit a perfect drive on No. 17, a nasty par four with a large, shallow green that sloped from front to back, fronted on the left by a lake and on the right by a bunker.

Her second shot would have to be just as good, long enough to clear the lip of the bunker, but not so long as to roll down the slope and off the back of the green. The wind was behind her, making it even harder.

Pat went through her routine, visualized the shot she wanted, and hit what she later described as a "career 6-iron, pure as the driven snow." It landed softly on the green and stopped fifteen feet past the hole. She had an uphill right-to-left putt, and she hit it aggressively. It was her margin of victory.

She was back.

. . .

PAT WENT ON to do almost exactly as she had told me she hoped she would in 1995. She limited her stints on the road to three or four weeks. She finished eleventh on the money list. She was in the top ten nearly a dozen times. She made a run at the U.S. Open. And she kept her life in balance.

Now, in her mid-forties, she's taken up weight training during the weeks she's not on the circuit. She tells me she feels stronger than she did when she started as a professional.

I think the autumn of her career may turn out to be an Indian summer.

No. 17

....

How Claude Williamson Got from

Stumpy Lake to the Cascades

....
....
....

WHEN A GOLFER I KNOW NAMED CLAUDE WILLIAMSON WALKED ONTO THE first tee for a quarterfinal match in the Virginia Senior Amateur championship last summer, he had already come a very long way.

The challenges he faced that morning were formidable. First of all, the tournament was being played on the Cascades course at the Homestead, up in the mountains in Hot Springs.

The Cascades is one of American golf's classic courses. It started hosting USGA national tournaments back in 1928. The fairways are narrow and canted, the greens are slick, and there's a creek in play on half the holes. It demands a good strategy, a confident swing, and a lot of patience.

More important to Claude, his opponent was Moss Beecroft, a man whose lineage in Virginia golf is almost as long and distinguished as the Homestead's. Moss had been playing and winning tournaments on courses like the Cascades for years. He was the defending champion.

But the challenges posed by Moss Beecroft and the Cascades, Claude might have said, were small in comparison to those he had surmounted just to become good enough to be there.

• • •

CLAUDE WILLIAMSON GREW up in Virginia's Tidewater area, but he never set foot on a golf course as a boy. He graduated from Virginia Tech with a degree in chemistry and went into the Army. The Army sent him to New York City, where it had a medical laboratory. He married, lived in Queens, and commuted to Manhattan.

There have probably been hundreds of Virginians who played golf as youngsters, moved to New York, and had to give up the game. There have no doubt been thousands of New Yorkers who never played as youngsters, moved to Virginia, and took it up. But Claude may be the only Virginian who's ever moved to New York City and taken the game up there. One Christmas, his wife bought him a set of irons. He embarked on his golfing career at twenty-four.

Like thousands of other New York golfers, Claude and a friend took to rising well before dawn on weekend mornings and heading out to a scruffy public course in Brooklyn, where they stood on line for a tee time. He took no lessons. He hit the ball, chased it, and felt frustrated. His scores were usually between 110 and 120.

When he left the Army, he moved back to Virginia, into a neighborhood where a lot of men played golf, getting together on weekends for a game and some beer. Claude soon joined them. They played at public courses in the Norfolk area, places like Lake Wright, Suffolk County, and Stumpy Lake. This was where his golfing education began.

He started taking lessons from an old touring pro named Claude King. His form improved, and he began shooting in the low 90s and high 80s.

Then he started playing at a course called the Bide-A-Wee

Golf Club, owned by another old pro named Chandler Harper. The caliber of players at Bide-A-Wee was a notch higher. Claude Williamson kept taking occasional lessons and practicing, and within a few years his handicap was down into single digits.

He had discovered, more or less by good fortune, several of the secrets to improvement. He took lessons and paid attention. He practiced a couple of times a week after work. He recognized that improvement was a long-term process. Most important, he did what he could to surround himself with players who challenged him to get better.

Claude's progress into the 70s demonstrates some hopeful truths for golfers who take up the game as adults and find themselves on public courses, unable to break 100.

It's true that they start out way behind those fortunate enough to have learned the game as kids. But it's also true that they have no bad memories weighing them down. They don't remember years of missed putts, sliced drives, and misery. They have no bad habits.

They haven't formed a fixed picture of themselves as golfers. I see a lot of people who have played golf for a while and stagnated. They see themselves as congenital 80s shooters, or 90s shooters. They put limits on themselves.

Claude didn't.

He recognized early on that he had to work on both his physical skills and his mind, and he was open to tips that would help him think better around the course.

One day he was playing with Chandler Harper at Bide-A-Wee. Claude hit a bad shot, and he started cussing himself.

"Claude, what's your handicap?" Harper asked.

"Seven," Claude replied.

"Well, after you've hit seven bad shots, then you can get upset with yourself," Harper said.

Claude remembered that advice, and he followed it for years.

He would count his bad shots and remind himself that he had no right to get angry until they exceeded his handicap. Not coincidentally, he found that this started to happen later and later in his rounds.

He discovered that he could improve his swing mechanics by watching television. At first, he would watch televised tournaments. He'd observe the positions that good players got into at various stages of their swings. And he would try to copy these positions.

Then he ran across a swing video by Al Geiberger and decided to make that his model. He got a video camera and taped his own swing. Then he'd play Geiberger's tape on one television and his own on another and watch them simultaneously. He tried to match Geiberger's takeaway, hand position, follow-through, and tempo.

I don't recommend this kind of use of videotape for everyone. Some people look at themselves on tape and say, "I can't believe my swing is that bad." The tape undermines their confidence. Others, like Claude, find it helps them. The important thing was that he found something that worked for him, that didn't confuse him, and he stuck with it.

As a result, his handicap continued to fall, until he was just about a scratch player. It had taken him twenty years of consistent effort to get there, but he made it.

At around the same time, Claude moved to Charlottesville, which is where I got to know him. We competed in some city tournaments. We talked a few times, casually, about the kinds of attitudes that would help him continue to improve.

I ran into him just last summer at a tournament, when he asked me to autograph his copy of *Golf Is Not a Game of Perfect*. Claude was later kind enough to say that the book had helped him.

First, it reminded him of the importance of a pre-shot routine.

After reading it and thinking about what worked best for him, Claude had developed a mantra he called "aah," an acronym for "align, aim, and hit." That's as good a summary of any of the basic components of a good routine. He set his body up the same way every time. He picked his target and aimed at it. And without further ado, he swung.

Second, the book reminded him to pick out small targets. Claude had been in the habit of aiming at general vicinities, like the middle of the fairway. He started aiming at particular branches or bunker corners.

Third, the book reminded him to trust his swing when he played. If he hit a bad shot, rather than start to question his mechanics and try to fix them, Claude resolved to try harder to stick with his mental pre-shot routine.

Finally, the book refreshed his memory of what Chandler Harper had told him years ago about accepting the results of any shot, regardless of what happens to it. He stopped letting missed putts make him angry and affect his concentration on the next tee.

As a result of all these things, he got a little more consistent.

CLAUDE FINISHED READING *Golf Is Not a Game of Perfect* just as he was getting ready to leave for the Homestead and the Virginia Senior Amateur.

He had not been able to put in the practice time he usually does before an important tournament. Claude works for an insurance company. Six weeks before the tournament started, his company had been asked to take over the University of Virginia employees' disability insurance policy. The ensuing deluge of work had meant he'd had little time to practice. In fact, Claude had had to withdraw from the State Amateur because he couldn't get away.

I've seen, quite often, that such circumstances can actually help a player who is fundamentally well-prepared. Given a lot of time to practice, this kind of player can work too hard to be ready for a particular tournament. He can get too tight and too perfectionistic.

But if circumstances prevent him from doing a lot of pretournament practicing, this kind of player can lower his expectations, get looser, and actually play better. It depends on the individual.

When he arrived at the Homestead, Claude followed another tip he'd gotten from *Golf Is Not a Game of Perfect* and walked the course backward. Looking at holes from green to tee, he could better see the optimal angle of approach to each green and the optimal landing area for each drive.

He could also see where the slope of a fairway meant that the landing area was in fact more restricted than it looked from the tee. On the first two holes, for instance, the fairways fell sharply from left to right. That meant that a drive down the right side might bounce into trouble. He brought along a yardage book and marked it up with a pencil, based on the way he wanted to play each hole.

Claude shot 75 and 78 in the stroke-play qualifying segment of the tournament and finished eighth. He closed out his first two matches 7 and 5. That brought him to the quarterfinals against Moss Beecroft.

It's often tough for a player without credentials of one kind or another to face a player with extensive credentials. It might be the club championship; you're the last player into the top flight and you go up against the guy who's won it the past three years. It could be the U.S. Senior Open and you're Larry Laoretti competing against Jack Nicklaus. The problem is the same.

If it's someone you've never played before, you had better

not let paper credentials beat you. You need to think that you're better than he is until he proves otherwise.

I sometimes ask tournament golfers who tell me they don't think they can win. "Well, who is it you think is going to win? Who do you believe in more than yourself?"

It's a waste of time to make a commitment to becoming good, to practice consistently, and then go out and believe in someone else more than you believe in yourself. At the very least, a player has to enter a tournament with the attitude that he's better than anyone else until someone proves otherwise. Put the burden of proof on the competition.

If it's someone who's beaten you the past ten times you've played, you have to believe that you can bring a new attitude and, hence, a new game, to the match. Maybe you lost with your old game and old attitude. But that doesn't mean you will with your new ones.

Moreover, you can remind yourself that you are your real opponent. **If you can win the battle with your mind and emotions and play your best game, then you can't really lose**. You may simply find out that on this particular day, someone had a better golf game than you had, or that you ran out of holes.

Claude worked on thinking that way. He told himself that Moss Beecroft had only fourteen clubs, the same as he did. But he didn't get much sleep that night.

And he didn't have the chance to build up confidence on the practice tee before the match. The Homestead's practice range is a long way from the Cascades course's first tee, and the match began early in the morning. Claude went to the tee without hitting any warm-up balls.

This is a problem a lot of amateurs encounter. They have a match they badly want to win. But they can't get to the course in time to warm up. Or the course doesn't have a practice tee.

The best way to handle this situation is to find time to visualize the tee shot you want to hit. Take a lot of practice swings and make sure your muscles are as loose as you can make them. Pick up a club you can trust; if your driver has been balky of late, or the hole is tight, it might be best to leave the driver in the bag for a few holes. Concentrate on your target and your pre-shot routine. And no matter what happens, don't assume that the first tee shot, good or bad, will have any influence on the shots you play thereafter.

Claude had been hitting his driver well, so he pulled that club out of the bag and hit it exactly where his game plan specified. He hit his approach shot to six feet. Though he didn't make the birdie putt, he easily parred the hole. Beecroft bogeyed it.

Something like this frequently happens when a player with credentials meets a player without credentials. The favorite can come to the first tee complacent. If the underdog is ready to play from the first stroke, he can often jump out to a lead.

They halved the next ten holes. No. 12 is one of the toughest holes on the Cascades, a 476-yard downhill par four. The creek crosses the fairway and then runs along the left side all the way to the green.

Claude, still with the honor, busted his best drive down the middle, about 210 yards from the green. Beecroft reached back for a little extra distance and pushed his tee shot to the right, into the rough. He couldn't reach the green, and made bogey. Claude hit a 7-wood, which he carries in place of a 2-iron, almost stiff. He coddled the six-foot birdie putt, knowing that he needed only a par. He made the tap-in and he was two up.

They halved the next four holes with pars. No. 17 at the Cascades is a great par five to play toward the end of a tight match. It's 491 yards, a dogleg left, with the creek running all the way down the right side of the hole. It's reachable, by experts, with two great shots. But the risks are high.

Claude, with the advantage of being dormie, hit a driver down the middle. Beecroft hit his drive into the creek on the right. Claude made a routine par, and the match was over.

The tournament, of course, wasn't over. Claude still had two matches to play; he warned himself not to start celebrating early. Despite a slight letdown in the semifinals, he won 3 and 1 again. And he won the final match 5 and 4.

It took Claude a while to appreciate fully what he'd done. Then he started to savor it. Claude had lifted himself, rung by rung, from the bottom of the ladder in Virginia golf to the top. The view from there was very satisfying.

Most dreams are attainable if the dreamer is ready to devote consistent, intelligent effort to them.

No. 18

How Tom Kite

Honors His Commitment

ONCE IN A WHILE, SOMEONE WILL APPROACH ME AT A GOLF TOURNAMENT or clinic and tell me what a relief it is to learn that he can become a first-class golfer just by changing the way he thinks.

Or someone out on the tour will come to me because he's heard that I help players get better just by changing the way they think.

They might even bring up an example, saying that they observed the way Tom Kite improved after he started working with me—just by changing the way he thinks.

I am at once flattered, embarrassed, and slightly irritated by this kind of compliment.

It's true that a lot of golfers who are presently averaging 95 could drop that average under 90 by improving their thinking: staying in the present, trusting their swings, picking out small targets, accepting the results of their shots, following intelligent routines and game plans.

They are weekend players who don't want to practice and who will be content to break 85 or 80 on occasion. I'm happy to be able to help them develop that kind of game to its fullest by thinking effectively.

But there are others who have reached that stage and are tired of it. They want to press ahead, to test themselves. They shoot 85 and would like to regularly shoot 75. They shoot 75 and they think it should be 69. They want to play well consistently. Some of them, unfortunately, would like to believe that all this requires is a psychological massage, a quick and easy change in their thinking. This bothers me, both because it's inaccurate and because it undervalues the work done by players who do improve.

The difference between a dream and a fantasy is commitment.

I wish that I could take all of the fantasizers with me some day to watch Tom Kite practice. Then they might begin to understand the commitment required to find out how good they can be.

A typical day at home in Austin during the golf season begins with Tom rising early and seeing his children off to school. Then he goes to the course. He stretches, carefully and thoroughly.

He'll hit wedges and work his way up through his irons and his woods. Then he'll work on his short game some more. This might take two or three hours. He's not counting.

Nor is he paying much attention to the weather. If it's a sunny day in July, it might be 98 degrees out on the practice tee. He will stay out there until sweat plasters the shirt to his back and the trousers to his thighs, take a short break to towel off and drink some water, and then practice some more.

In fact, there is a side of Tom that relishes the heat, a side that is thinking, "Good. It's so hot that a lot of guys won't practice. But I'll build up strength, discipline, and endurance, and the next time the U.S. Open is at Oakmont or Congressional or someplace where it sizzles in the summer, I'll have the advantage."

Then Tom might play a round, but he'll play it competitively, trying to simulate tournament conditions as closely as possible.

After the round, he'll go back to the practice tee and work on whatever facets of his game did not meet his standards when he played.

Up until this point, I could be describing the practice regimens of any number of first-rate players.

What separates Tom from the rest is the quality of his practice, not the quantity. Some players just beat balls. They work, but they don't improve.

Some players even set themselves up for failure as they practice. They fear failure. Even more, they fear the guilt they will feel if they fail without having practiced. So they hit balls until dark, thinking subconsciously that no one, including themselves, will be able to say they missed the cut or lost their tour cards because they didn't work. Players who fear failure generally play with fear, and consequently generally play badly.

Some people work hard, but they are unable to see themselves as successful, as winners. Their hard work never bears fruit.

Tom does not fear failure. He hates to lose, and he loves to win, but he's not afraid of failure. His love of winning drives his practice habits. He doesn't see practice as an exercise in self-denial or sacrifice. He sees it as an integral part of the process of improvement and winning. He sees himself as a winner.

He knows that the competition is working hard; some are getting better. He will do whatever is necessary to be as prepared as he can be, because that is how he maximizes his chances of winning.

To improve, a player must practice in the right way, working on both his swing and his mind.

As he practices, Tom is constantly challenging his mind and his creativity in an effort to do both.

A lot of this he picked up as a boy, first in Dallas and then in Austin. His father belonged to River Lake Country Club in Dallas, where Tom first started to play. And I use the word "play" advisedly. Golf was never work for Tom or the other kids. They spent all summer long at the course and on the practice tee. But it was always a game.

The boys constantly invented contests to amuse themselves. Who could hit it highest? Who could hit it lowest? Who could hit it the shortest distance using a full swing with a driver? Who could hit it farthest with a wedge? Who could slice it the most? Or hook it the most?

On the golf course, there were more games. The boys might call each other's shots. Tom's opponent could stand on the tee and tell him that his drive had to start off over the right rough and draw into the fairway. Then Tom might make his opponent hit a 90-yard bump and run onto the green.

Some of these games might seem silly and even harmful. To win a long wedge contest, for example, you have to learn how to blade the ball. It's not a shot you'd likely want to hit on the course. But it teaches control of the club. It teaches a boy to envision a shot and then trust his brain and body to hit it. It teaches how to play under pressure. It trains both the swing and the mind.

In fact, it often strikes me that adults would be better off if they let kids teach *them* how to practice, rather than the other way around. Kids are more creative and instinctive.

In Tom's case, the child was indeed father to the man. He still plays games that train his swing and his mind concurrently. When he's on the range, he reminds me in many ways of city kids playing basketball—playful, competitive, joyful. This does not mean he's one of the guys who wander around the tee, kibitzing. He's there to accomplish something, and his attitude toward people who drop by to schmooze is the same as a businessman's might be toward someone who barged into a business meeting to chat. He doesn't welcome it.

But people see this concentration and they mistake it for something robotic, even obsessive. In fact, just the opposite is true. On the practice tee, Tom might deliberately hit two big slices and then pure the next ball, just to know he can do it. When I'm around, he asks me to give him challenges. I might tell him to start a driver at a tree in the distance and draw it eight yards. Then start a 5-iron at a bush by the edge of the range and hit a high cut. Hit a wedge over a tree or punch a 7-iron under a branch and make it stop. Then take ten balls and aim for a pin sixty-five yards away. Hit the pin at least once, and I buy dinner. Miss with all ten, and dinner's on Tom.

He rarely buys dinner.

Tom finds ways to inject fun—and tension—into short-game practice. He'll seek out a thin, sandy patch of worn-out grass, drop some balls, and hit lob wedges to a high pin. From such a lie, his misses look awful, plopping weakly into the bunker or flying low over the green like frightened quail. But he knows that when he can handle this drill, he is hitting the ball precisely. Sometimes it amazes me just how precisely. When he practices putts, I ask him to tell me which side of the hole the ball will enter, and how fast. He does. I have seen him stand eight to ten feet from the hole on a flat section of the practice green and chip in eight consecutive balls. With a sand wedge. Without scuffing the green.

Tom also constantly tries to simulate the pressure he will feel in competition. In 1993, during his four-ball match at the Ryder Cup, Tom hit a marvelous 3-wood to the green of the short par-four tenth hole, a shot that had to fade precisely over a stream, between two large trees, and hold a small green. It was a pivotal shot in securing the match for the United States. It was a shot that Tom had practiced over and over on the range. And every time he did, he would tell himself that he was standing on the tee with the Ryder Cup on the line, the European crowd quietly eager to see him fail, the television cameras focused on him, his partner anxious. In short, he tried to experience all the emotions and stress he would feel in the actual competition. When the big moment came, he had a feeling of déjà vu, a feeling of confidence.

MOST OF ALL, Tom's commitment is such that he treats setbacks as goads to get better.

If he could play one shot from his career over again, it probably would be the ball he hit into the swollen waters of the creek on the fifth hole of Rochester's Oak Hill Country Club during the last round of the 1989 U.S. Open. Going into that day, he had recorded masterful rounds of 67, 69, and 69. He led by a stroke over Scott Simpson and three over Curtis Strange. Mentally, he felt as sharp as he ever had.

The fatal shot at No. 5 was a block to the right. After the penalty, Tom reached the green of the par four in four and, upset, three-putted from twelve feet. The Open slipped away.

As soon as the tournament was over, Tom reflected honestly on his mental state at the time he hit the ball. Had his mind been in the present? He thought that it had. Had he believed in the shot? Yes. Had he doubted himself in some way? No. Mentally, he had done everything he was supposed to do.

There was only one other conclusion to reach. His swing had broken down.

It was not, in fact, the first time that he had blocked a ball right of right under pressure. Earlier that year, he had almost lost at Bay Hill when he put his approach to the eighteenth green into a lake.

Tom looked at film and talked with two teaching professionals he trusted, Chuck Cook and John Rhodes. He decided that under pressure his swing was prone to deliver the clubhead to the ball on an inside-to-out path that was too pronounced. (This sometimes happened on the range too, but you tend to forget those.) It was the same problem that plagued Greg Norman and Johnny Miller at certain stages of their careers.

Tom and his teachers agreed to make a significant swing change, widening his stance and flattening his swing plane, so that he could square the clubface with his body rather than his arms.

A lot of players of Tom's stature would be chary of making this kind of change, knowing that their games might regress for a while. But Tom did not want the thought of possible blocked shots hanging over him. He was still on a quest to see how good he could be, and if that quest required a swing change, so be it.

He started working on the change during the off-season at the end of 1989. He spent countless hours on practice tees. As Tom says, he doesn't watch the clock when he's having fun. For him, improvement is fun. He enjoys nothing more than the feeling of getting better.

He practiced his new swing into 1990, and in spurts, it worked very well. But just as he thought he was getting it down, he overdid it a bit by getting through the ball too much with his upper body. And because he had never played with this flaw, his misses went everywhere. So at the end of the 1991 season, he went back to the range for more refinement of his swing.

Finally, early in the 1992 season, it all fell into place. Golf started to seem easy. If he wanted to hit it high, he hit it high. If he wanted to turn it right-to-left, he turned it. His wedges were sharp. He putted confidently. And he felt no threat of disastrous misses like the one at Oak Hill hanging over his head. He won the BellSouth Classic in Atlanta, his first title in sixteen months. Heading into the early summer and the U.S. Open at Pebble Beach, he felt like a pilot who has broken through the clouds to find smooth air and a tailwind. Everything was copacetic.

Pebble Beach is one of Tom's favorite courses. He'd won the Bing Crosby there; he holds the course record. Pebble Beach embodies the kind of challenge and tradition he respects most in golf. It is no coincidence that players of the caliber of Jack Nicklaus and Tom Watson had won the previous opens at Pebble Beach.

But for some reason, at Pebble Beach Tom found that his swing had gone slightly awry. It was nothing awful, except by the high standards Tom had set for himself, particularly in the previous few weeks. He could not consistently get the ball to start on his intended line and go right-to-left. Instead, he was hitting a ball that started a little left and faded slightly.

A lot of people who had spent the time and effort Tom did to modify their swings would have reacted by spending the whole week trying to find that tight, beautiful little draw again. Worse, they might have persuaded themselves that there was no way they could play well without it. Tom, fortunately, knew better.

We talked on Tuesday night, two days before the tournament started. We agreed that he had to decide that he could win the U.S. Open without his A-plus swing, that he could use the swing that he had that week, plus his mind and his short game, to find a way to prevail. And he did. He played that whole week with a swing that felt far less than perfect, not the one he had practiced and worked on. Of the sixty-six players who made the cut, fifty-three hit more fairways than Tom; thirty-one hit more greens. No one took fewer strokes.

A rundown of Tom's final round shows how this was possible.

Tom arrived at the course Sunday morning one stroke behind the leader, Gil Morgan. The practice tee at Pebble Beach is inland a bit from the ocean and protected from the brunt of the wind, so Tom did not immediately realize what the conditions would be like on that day. He warmed up with his long clubs, then made sure to spend some time practicing flop shots at the chipping and pitching green the USGA had installed for the Open. Then he went to the putting green.

There, he felt the wind start to freshen and blow hard off the Pacific, up to 30 miles an hour. He saw the sun shining, and he realized that the combination of sun and wind would dry the greens until they had the resilience of billiard tables. It would be a brutal day for scoring. The wind would affect every shot. Some greens would be nearly impossible to hold, and a lot of pins would be inaccessible.

Tom left his woods in the bag for his tee shot at No. 1, a 378-yard par four that gets a round at Pebble Beach off to a gentle start. He hit a 3-iron into the fairway and a 9-iron to the green. He poured in his birdie putt, a breaking 20-footer.

Oh, boy, he thought, *this is going to be fun.*

Any premature jubilation was tempered on the next few holes. At No. 2, a short par five where good players count on birdies, he hit a mediocre pitch to the green for his third shot and missed his putt. His par felt like a bogey. Despite being one under, he felt as if he hadn't gained anything on the field.

On No. 3, though, he got an inkling of what the field would be doing that day. His playing partner, Mark Brooks, four-putted from about twelve feet. The greens were that treacherous. Tom made a routine par.

He got into trouble himself by being a little aggressive on No. 4, a short par four that is the last of the easier, inland holes. The wind caught his tee shot and pushed it a few feet into the rough. Nevertheless, Tom elected to shoot at the pin, which was cut in the back right corner. His pitching wedge from the thick grass jumped a little, landed on the back of the green, and bounced like a basketball into a small bunker behind the green.

The ball settled on a downslope, and Tom faced the kind of penalizing situation that characterizes the U.S. Open—a sand shot from a downhill lie onto a crusty little green that sloped sharply away from him. There was no way to stop the ball close to the pin; he did well to keep it on the green, forty-five feet away. He then compounded the error with a poor putt that he left four feet short. His six left him one over par for the day.

This was perhaps the critical moment in Tom's round. A lot of players might have started feeling sorry for themselves, thinking that the USGA had tricked up the course. Tom could sympathize with that point of view. He was not happy, and as he passed his wife, Christy, on the way to the fifth tee, he said, "Well, it looks like the USGA has really done it to us today."

But he did not succumb to self-pity or anger. Nor did he think about what had happened at almost the same point in the final round in 1989 at Oak Hill. He didn't stop worrying that he was going to let another Open slip away. He reminded himself that based on what had happened to Brooks and him, there were going to be a lot of disasters during the final round. Everyone would suffer. He had to be patient.

Trying to gauge the wind at No. 5, a par three, he came off his 5-iron a bit and hit the ball into a right-hand bunker. When he reached it, he saw that the ball was buried in the sand.

"Oh, man," he said to himself. "I've just made double-bogey from a bunker at No. 4, and now I've got another bunker shot."

But he dragged his mind away from No. 4 and back into the present, hit a great explosion, and stopped the ball eight feet from the hole. Then he hit his par-saving putt into the heart of the hole.

There isn't much room for spectators at the fifth hole, and television rarely covers it. So when people talk about Tom's round at Pebble Beach, they rarely mention this hole. But the two short shots he hit to save his par at No. 5 were as important as any he struck that day.

At No. 6, Pebble Beach turns toward the ocean, into the teeth of the wind. Tom hit two beautiful wood shots and still barely made it to the top of the hill at the par-five sixth. He needed a knock-down 6-iron third shot to cover the last 115 yards to a green that's reachable in two on calm days.

He faced a twenty-foot putt, one that normally would have been very fast. But he realized that the wind would slow it down, and he gave it a firm stroke. The ball was going a little faster than he'd wanted, but it dove into the cup like a rat going into its hole. He was back to even par.

The tiny 113-yard seventh presented a harrowing shot. It's at the tip of a promontory, with an elevated tee. The wind was howling off the ocean. The only way to hit the green would have been to hit the ball out over the water and trust the wind to bring it back. The approximate aim point would almost have to be Yokohama. One player among the last thirty that day pulled the shot off.

Tom hit another 6-iron on a hole that is generally no more than a sand wedge shot, trying to keep it low, under the wind. But from the elevated tee, that was impossible. He watched the wind catch the ball and drive it left, left of the bunker, into thick rough by the eighth tee.

He faced his next shot calmly. The wind, directly in his face now, would help him this time, holding the shot and helping it land softly. He had been practicing his flop shot all week just for a moment like this. He swung confidently and lofted the ball over the bunker. It landed on the green, rolled directly to the hole, and fell in.

He did not celebrate. He breathed a sigh of relief, knowing how much hard golf he had yet to play.

At No. 8, the classic par four that spans a Pacific inlet, he faced a club selection problem. Normally, he hit a 3-wood to the landing area about 265 yards out in the fairway. But the gale behind him suggested that a 3-wood might be too much. So might a 4-wood, which would get up into the wind. A 3-iron seemed right. Then an even harder gust blew in from the ocean.

"Mike," Tom said to Mike Carrick, his caddie. "Do you think a 4-iron would be enough?"

"Maybe it is," Mike said.

It was. Tom blew the 4-iron 260 yards up the fairway into perfect position. Then he hit a beautiful 8-iron over the cliffs and brine and into the green. It landed just short of the pin and caromed as high as the flag. He wound up in the rough behind the green.

It left him much the same little flop shot he'd had at No. 7, and he hit it almost as well. He made a four-foot putt for his par.

No. 9 is a long par four, strung along the edge of a cliff, playing even longer because of the wind. Tom hit a fine drive, but the gale gave him a tough club choice. He wanted to hit a 4-wood to the green, but he was afraid of what the wind would do if he got the ball up in the air, which he tends to do with his 4-wood. So he opted instead to try to hit a low hook with his 3-iron. It's always tough to hit a shot when a player is in doubt about club selection. But at Pebble Beach in a 30-mile-per-hour gale, there are no easy club choices. Tom blocked the 3-iron right, into a patch of gnarly kikuyu grass halfway down the cliff to the beach. He was fortunate enough that a marshal saw where the ball went, or he might not have found it.

He had two choices. Since the cliffs and beach play as a lateral hazard, he could penalize himself a stroke and drop the ball forty yards or so in front of the green; or he could try to hit it out of the kikuyu. He had enormous confidence in the 62-degree Hogan wedge he'd been using for all his recovery shots that day, and he blasted this one out of the thicket and onto the green. He made five. But, as he told Mike as they walked off the green, "some bogies are better than others."

At No. 10, which wends its way further along the cliff, he pulled his drive left, conscious of the close brush with disaster he had survived on No. 9. His lie was terrible, and he could only hack a 7-iron out into the fairway. But he hacked it to the perfect yardage for his lob wedge, sixty-eight yards. He knocked the pitch stiff and made par.

At No. 11, with the wind finally behind him, he drove long and had only a sand wedge to the green. He knew better, this time, than to shoot for the pin. To reach the pin, he would have had to clear a bunker, and a shot that cleared the bunker would likely not hold the green. So he played left of the bunker, to the middle of the green, leaving himself twenty feet away but safely on. His putt almost went in. As he walked off the green he reminded himself that in the prevailing weather conditions, pars would be more than adequate. A remarkable number of players that day failed to break 80.

At No. 12, a par three, with the wind blowing fiercely from left to right, he took a 4-iron, closed the face a little, and tried to hit a big hook. The ball started out at the left edge of the green; on a calm day it might have hooked twenty yards left. But the wind blew it twenty yards right, onto the green about thirty feet right of the hole. The crowd around the green exploded with applause as if he had knocked it right up against the pin.

"Listen to that," Tom told Mike. "No one's hit this green for a long time."

He was right. Behind the twelfth green, he got a look at a leader board. He was the only player in the field under par.

Tom had always liked the green at No. 12. Over the years, in various tournaments, he'd made a number of birdies on it. With those thoughts in mind, he stroked his putt and holed it.

The crowd, of course, erupted again. He walked to the thirteenth tee feeling, as he said later, "super good about everything."

He parred No. 13 and then started down the long fourteenth, an uphill par five. Normally, the second shot at No. 14 is a layup, designed to give a player his most comfortable wedge shot for the approach to the green.

At this point, he remembered a chance encounter he had had the night before with two friends from Austin. Tom and Christy had been walking in Carmel after dinner, when they bumped into Lance and Hailey Hughes, who had come to California to watch the tournament.

They had sat by the fourteenth green most of the third round, watching golfer after golfer try to pitch on from ninety or one hundred yards, a pitch that had to clear a yawning bunker in front of the green. Invariably, their pitches either came up short in the bunker or hit the hardened green and kicked off the back and into the rough. That, in fact, had happened to Tom in the third round.

The only players who had held the green in three, Lance said, were the ones who tried to reach it in two and left themselves only a chip shot.

Remembering this, Tom took out his 3-wood and tried to hit it right of the bunker and long. He pulled it a bit and landed in the left rough, close to the green but with the bunker to negotiate.

He flopped the ball onto the green and stopped it two feet from the hole. He told me later that it never crossed his mind that he would hit anything but a great shot.

The birdie at No. 14 gave him a substantial lead. He was at

five under par; he didn't realize at the time that Jeff Sluman was having a good round and would finish at one under. He felt in control. He'd gotten past the worst holes on the golf course.

I don't recommend that players look at leader boards, although a lot of them do. They tend to distract players, to break their concentration on the shot at hand. For the leader in a major championship, that concentration is hard enough to keep. The mobile television crews are taking pictures of the grass where his ball lies. The crowds are yelling and screaming support as if this were a coronation instead of a golf tournament. It's hard not to start thinking about the people you'll thank when they hand you the trophy.

But Tom had looked at the leader boards and knew were he stood: If he played solid golf on the remaining four holes, the tournament was his. He had to take in that information without letting it change the way he'd been thinking up till that point.

At No. 15, he hit a good tee shot with his 3-wood, but he hooked it a little too much, trying to hold it against the wind. It landed in the left rough. He knocked a great iron shot to the edge of the green, stroked a 40-foot putt to within six inches, and made his par.

The crowd was roaring, and for a few seconds Tom was tempted to celebrate with them. But he reminded himself that he had three tough holes left to play, gave them a smile and a tip of his hat, and tried to focus on business.

At No. 16, still contending with the wind, he hit another 3-wood into the right rough. His 6-iron approach caught the back of the green and rolled off. He hit his chip shot a little heavy, and then hit a mediocre putt. He made bogey. He was down to four under.

No. 17 presented him with yet another of Pebble Beach's club selection dilemmas. The pin was in the left side of the back half of the hourglass-shaped green, about as far from the tee as it could get. The wind was blowing so strongly in his face that he thought he might need a driver to reach it. But a driver, if the wind slacked off as he swung, could fly the green and put him on the one place that could jeopardize the tournament, the beach.

He opted for a 3-wood, and put the ball into the bunker that fronts the green. He got a bad break. The ball came to rest on the left edge of the bunker, on a side slope. He would have an awkward stance, with one foot out of the sand and one foot in. The wind was in his face, and he had a long carry. Double-bogey was certainly a possibility.

Oh, man, he thought. *Why couldn't I have gotten a plain vanilla bunker shot?*

It was time for yet one more recovery shot with his wedge, and he hit a good one, not giving himself time to think about what might happen if he chunked it or bladed it. It landed on the green about ten feet from the pin. He missed the putt, but all he needed, at this stage, was a bogey.

This putt was the only mental error he made on the finishing holes. Thinking he had the tournament in hand, he lost his concentration. But he turned that lapse into a positive factor. He used it to remind himself to concentrate exclusively on his routine as he played the critical tee shot at No. 18.

All week long Tom had been hitting a 3-wood off the tee at No. 18, the famous par five that stretches 548 yards along the ocean's edge. But his last three shots with that club had failed to find short grass. He wanted a club he could hit confidently.

"What do you think about a driver?" he asked Mike.

Mike, probably trying to avoid looking at the ocean, gulped and said, "Yeah, that's fine."

Tom fell back on the pre-shot habits he had practiced for so many years. He picked out his target. He confined himself to one swing thought: *slow.*

He took the club back as slowly as he could. On tape, later, he would see that there was nothing particularly slow about the swing. But he felt like a figure in a slow-motion movie. He swung.

"That's a tee-picker-upper," Mike said.

It was. It was the kind of drive that's hit so well that the golfer doesn't have to watch and see what happens to it. He can bend over, pick up the tee, and start walking.

It was straight, and it was long. He could have, if he had had a big lead or was a stroke behind, gone for the green in two. He laid up with a 5-iron, leaving himself once again with seventy yards left to the hole—the perfect distance for his lob wedge. When he knocked his third onto the green, he knew that his long quest for a major championship was over.

His triumph demonstrated so many things. It showed the importance of the short game. Even though he missed a lot of fairways and greens, he was able to play well because of his wedge and putter. He hit ten lob wedges during his round.

It showed the importance of staying in the present. Except for a few minor lapses, Tom would tell me later, his round had no past and no future. He was always thinking of the shot at hand. He never once thought about what had happened to him in 1989 or all the other times he had been in contention at a major championship.

It showed the importance of commitment: commitment to improvement, commitment to doing whatever you can do to win.

For a period of about a year, until the spring of 1993, Tom was the best player in the world. He won the Los Angeles Open. At the Bob Hope, he nearly lapped the field, setting a scoring record that still stands, 35 under par for ninety holes.

Then, on an off day, he took his kids to an amusement park. One of them jumped on his back to see a passing attraction. The next morning, Tom's back felt wooden and sore. Eventually, he went to a doctor and had an MRI exam. He had three bulging disks—one, perhaps, caused by the accident with his child, and the other two much older.

Tom tried to continue playing. The next month, I flew down to Augusta to stay with Tom during the Masters. Normally, when he invites me to meet him somewhere, he picks me up at the airport himself. But this time, his father met me, and I knew something was wrong.

We drove to a strip mall in Augusta, to the dark, dank little office of an acupuncturist. We found Tom lying on a table with sixty or eighty needles sticking out of him—from his torso, his ears, even around his eyes. He turned over and there were just as many stuck in various places on his backside.

That was how much he wanted to play in the Masters.

The acupuncture did little good, and he did not play well in the tournament.

Tom went home for a while to work on his rehabilitation. No one knew then whether the back injury would be chronic. But I knew that if there was any way to prevent that, Tom would find it. He would refuse to let the injury become an excuse, refuse to pity himself. He would seek out the best advice he could find. And whatever those advisers prescribed, he would do. He would take control of the health of his back. He would attack the rehabilitation process. No matter how many hours a day they told him to exercise, he would. He would even find a way to look at the injury as a blessing, as a goad to get stronger and fitter and thereby prolong his career.

But the road back has been long and daunting, even for Tom. His back healed, but when it did, his command of his game was not quite the same. He didn't win for the rest of 1993 or the following year. And 1995 was, by Tom's standards, a terrible year. He didn't win a tournament. He finished 104th on the money list.

There were reasons. He and Christy were building their dream house. That distracted him. He didn't put in quite the same amount of time practicing, particularly with his wedges. He lost his patience at times and let his frustration affect his game.

But Tom has had down years before. And each time, he's discovered and rediscovered that he intensely dislikes playing poorly and will do anything he can to get back on top.

When the season ended, he looked forward to going home. He thought of the off months as a time for purging the traces of 1995 and rebuilding himself and his game for 1996.

In contrast to his post-1989 reconstruction period, Tom did not feel a need to change his swing. That, he thought, was solid.

Instead, he concentrated on his body and his mind. From Thanksgiving through Christmas, he planned to leave his clubs in the closet most of the time. But every day, he would be exercising—lifting weights, jogging, using the StairMaster. His routine varies each day, because he doesn't want to get bored with it. But there is always something. Winter, Tom feels, is when a player has to build up the strength and endurance he will need to carry him through the next season.

This is why the writers and commentators who have suggested Tom is simply over the hill at forty-six are wrong. Physically, he is in better shape now than he was in college. He weighs less, and he's stronger. He didn't lift weights until fairly recently. Now, like most players who want to be competitive, he's a firm believer in it.

And Tom will spend a lot of time in the office he's built in his new home, a sanctuary of dark wood paneling and warm memories. The walls are covered with memorabilia—magazine covers, photos, plaques, and trophies. They remind him of important milestones in his golf career and of the people who helped him achieve them.

The room has a television set, a VCR, and a cabinet that contains videotapes of every tournament Tom has won or played well in. He has a cassette called the "Tom Kite Highlight Film." He has another of the Tom Kite model swing.

I suggested that Tom compile the highlight tapes and watch them, because I have always felt that Tom was, at times, too demanding and judgmental of himself. Some of that he inherits from the upright work ethic of his father, who was a supervisor for the Internal Revenue Service. Mr. Kite was the kind of man who never stopped trying to improve the efficiency of the offices he managed. If his employees were doing 95 percent of their work properly, Mr. Kite worried about the remaining 5 percent and how to fix it. That was no doubt a good attitude for an IRS supervisor to have. But it will take a golfer only so far. A perfectionist, self-critical attitude can help someone become a good player. But it won't help him take the next step and become a great player, because once on the course, great players think more about what they can do well than about what they do poorly.

Tom started learning this in his boyhood from Harvey Penick, who relentlessly emphasized the positive aspects of every pupil's game. Tom learned more by watching the great players of the generation that preceded his—Arnold Palmer, Lee Trevino, and Gary Player, his boyhood idol. He noticed the way they carried themselves and talked.

But this was still something I thought Tom needed to work on when he and I first got together in 1984, just before the Doral tournament in Miami. We talked a lot about how effective persons know how to appreciate their own best attributes. They value their achievements. They acknowledge their shortcomings and they work to improve them, but they keep them in perspective.

Even the best golfers lose more tournaments than they win. And even when they win, they make mistakes. I told Tom that he had to realize that mortals attain perfection only fleetingly. The rest of the time, they are well advised to accept being human, to accept the fact that humans make mistakes. I told him not to forget that he is one of the best golfers on the planet even if he misses shots.

Tom won the 1984 Doral Open, beating Jack Nicklaus down the stretch. At eight o'clock the following morning he called me to thank me for my help. For a little while, he talked about how great it had felt to play well and beat a champion as great as Nicklaus.

Then he said, "God, I must have made a total fool of myself when I jumped up and threw my visor on the eighteenth green."

I laughed. "You son of a gun," I said. "If you can't have fun making birdie on four of the last five holes and rolling in a forty-footer on the eighteenth to beat Nicklaus, then you can't have fun. The world wants to watch you have fun playing golf!"

If Tom had a tendency to be critical of himself within twenty-four hours of one of the best days of his career, it's not hard to imagine how much playing badly gnaws at him. He works very hard to maintain the positive, optimistic attitude that Harvey Penick instilled in him when he was a boy.

That's what the tapes are intended to help him do. Seeing himself hit spectacularly good shots under pressure refreshes Tom's mind. It reminds him of how well he can play. As he says, "It's an ego boost in a sport where your ego needs a lot of boosting."

. . .

SO HE WILL watch the tapes, and lift the weights, and when the times comes to practice again, he will practice hard. That is the nature of his commitment.

Then he will return to the tour, and everyone in the golf world will be watching to see if he can come back. Tom once said that playing in a golf tournament is like walking out in front of the public buck naked. He feels as if he's vulnerable to every critic, every second-guesser. He does it because he loves the feeling he gets when he comes through. It is a feeling he never gets tired of.

But I think that whatever happens on the course, Tom cannot really fail. He does not, at the beginning of each year, set the standard goals for himself. He does not say that he wants to win a certain number of tournaments or dollars. He has dreams—dreams of winning major championships. And now, I'm sure, he dreams of being the playing captain who leads the United States to victory in the 1997 Ryder Cup.

His objective, every day, is the same: to do whatever he can to become the best player he can be. Because of the way he honors his commitment, Tom is bound to continue to succeed. When his career finally ends, maybe after the Senior Skins game in 2015, he'll be able to look back and take pleasure in something that he and some other fortunate people have learned: It's the striving that gives a person pleasure and satisfaction. Or, as Tom puts it, "I enjoy improving. Big time."

He will know that his commitment made him happy and content nearly all the days of his life.

That's the happiness I wish for every golfer.

Appendix

• To play golf as well as he can, a player must focus his mind tightly on the shot he is playing now, in the present.

• A player who is committed to the process of hitting good shots will never draw a club back until he knows where he wants the ball to go and believes that the club in his hands will send it there.

• Nearly all golfers would be better off if they forgot about the score as they played.

• A golfer cannot score as well as possible if he is thinking about swing mechanics as he plays.

• A golfer has to train his swing on the practice tee, then trust it on the course.

• In putting, the challenge is to make a free stroke to a specific target. Guiding, steering, or being too careful with a putting stroke are faults bred by doubt.

• A golfer's brain and nervous system perform best when they're focused on a small, precise target.

• The right choice is the decisive choice.

• Acceptance is critical after a bad shot. An angry player can't really execute a pre-shot mental routine.

• As long as the rules reward getting the ball in the hole in the fewest strokes, golf will be about playing well with the wedges and the putter.

• Sometimes, golfers forget that the object of the game is not to have a great swing, but to put the ball into the hole.

• The disease called the yips doesn't exist, except in the mind.

• Every individual goes through periods when he does a lot of the right things—practicing efficiently, thinking well—and gets no immediate tangible results. This is the point at which successful people bring to bear the powers of faith, patience, persistence, and will. Faith is the ability to believe without any tangible evidence.

• A conservative strategy joined to a cocky swing produces low scores. Reckless boldness joined to a doubtful swing is a formula for disaster.

• Athletes who become self-critical perfectionists are flirting with trouble.

• The best remedies for a golfing slump are putting things back in perspective, dwelling on the positive, looking for something good to happen—and rededication to the short game.

• It's not very important where you've been. Life is about where you're going.

• The optimal state of mind is something a player must work on patiently every day.

• It's not what happens to golfers, but how they choose to respond to what happens, that distinguishes champions.

• Which comes first, confidence or winning? The implication, in some minds, is that you can't win until you have confidence, and you can't get confidence until you've won. But if that were the case, no one would ever win for the first time. The fact is that the confidence required to win can be learned.

• The best way to introduce a kid to golf is casually.

• A child of almost any age can't spend too much time playing golf and practicing. But children burn out if they're doing it because someone requires it and they're not having fun.

• A golfer has to learn to compartmentalize. The happiest players are the ones who do.

• If you can win the battle with your mind and emotions and play your best game, then you can't really lose.

• Most dreams are attainable if the dreamer is ready to devote consistent, intelligent effort to them.

• The difference between a dream and a fantasy is commitment.

• To improve, a player must practice in the right way, working on both his swing and his mind.

Acknowledgments

ONCE AGAIN, WE HAVE BEEN BLESSED WITH MANY PEOPLE TO THANK. Every golfer featured in this book cheerfully contributed hours of time and candid recollections. We are in their debt.

Students and faculty in the Curry School of Education at the University of Virginia generously afforded time to research and complete the book.

Dominick Anfuso and Cassie Jones at Simon & Schuster provided encouragement and a title. Rafe Sagalyn, our literary agent, came up with the format. Guy Rotella, Jr., read the manuscript as it progressed and helped straighten out our syntax and clarify our thinking.

Finally, our families—Darlene and Casey Rotella and Ann, Peter, and Catherine Cullen, lovingly forgave the absences from domestic duties that the book required.

B.R. and B.C.
FEBRUARY 1996

About the Authors

DR. BOB ROTELLA, Director of Sports Psychology in the Curry School of Education at the University of Virginia, has been a consultant to some of the top golf organizations in the world, including PGA of America, the PGA Tour, the LPGA Tour, and the Senior LPGA Tour. A writer for and consultant to *Golf Digest,* he lives in Charlottesville, Virginia, with his wife, Darlene, and daughter, Casey.

BOB CULLEN is a journalist and a novelist. Since he began collaborating with Bob Rotella, he has reduced his handicap by nine strokes and broken 80 for the first time. He lives with his wife and children in Chevy Chase, Maryland.